BLOODY VICTORY

About the Authors

J.L. GRANATSTEIN is Professor of History at York University in Toronto. He has written or co-authored many highly acclaimed books, including *The Generals: The Canadian Army's Senior Commanders in the Second World War* and *Shadows of War, Faces of Peace: Canada's Peacekeepers.* He is the co-author, with Desmond Morton, of two best-selling books about Canada at war: *Marching to Armageddon* and *A Nation Forged in Fire.*

DESMOND MORTON, one of Canada's most widely read historians, is the Principal of Erindale College, University of Toronto. He is also the author of almost thirty books, including *When Your Number's Up: The Canadian Soldier in the First World War* and *Silent Battle: Canadian Prisoners of War in Germany 1914–1919*, and is one of the contributors to *The Illustrated History of Canada.*

BLOODY

CANADIANS AND THE D-DAY CAMPAIGN 1944

VICTORY

J.L. GRANATSTEIN   DESMOND MORTON

LESTER
PUBLISHING
LIMITED

Canadian Cataloguing in Publication Data

Morton, Desmond, 1937-
　　Bloody victory : Canadians and the D-Day campaign 1944

Authors in reverse order in previous ed.
Includes bibliographical references and index.
ISBN 1-895555-56-6

1. Canada.　Canadian Army — History — World War, 1939-1945.
2. World War, 1939-1945 — Campaigns — France — Normandy.
3. World War, 1939-1945 — Canada.　I. Granatstein, J.L., 1939- .
II. Title.

D756.5.N6G7　1994　　　940.54'2142　　　C93-095161-1

Design by Don Fernley
Maps by Geographics

Lester Publishing Limited
56 The Esplanade
Toronto, Ontario
Canada M5E 1A7

Printed and bound in Canada

94 95 96 97　5 4 3 2 1

Contents

For
Colonel Charles Perry Stacey
Canada's most distinguished military historian

Acknowledgements

The authors wish to acknowledge the assistance of the Canadian War Museum and the Canadian Museum of Civilization for making available the superb examples of Canadian war art reproduced here. The Directorate of History, National Defence Headquarters and the National Archives of Canada supplied the photographs. These, in turn, were the work of Canada's war photographers, who often risked their lives to capture these authentic images of our past: Harold G. Aikman, Ken Bell, Michael M. Dean, Frank I. Durbervill, D.I. Grant, Gilbert A. Milne and many others.

Kathie Hill and Clara Stewart patiently formatted, inputted and corrected successive versions of the typescript, while Phyllis Bruce and Gena Gorrell excised the worst barbarities of our prose. For the errors and infelicities that remain, blame us and invincible ignorance. Both of us know how deeply grateful authors should be to their families for being there and, with even greater thoughtfulness, making themselves scarce. Helping those we know best to understand what happened half a century ago has been the touchstone for all we did. If we succeed, they deserve the credit.

Preface

The young Canadian soldiers of 1944 are half a century older now. Time has been as remorseless an enemy as the *Hitlerjugend* snipers in the hedgerows of Normandy, and far more enduring. Some try to forget old battles. Others, their numbers shrinking annually, meet to relive good times and remember departed friends. And they wonder why their service to Canada is forgotten or is disparaged as mismanaged folly.

With the passage of so many years, only a handful of Canadians do remember. Two generations have grown up without war. Canada's armed forces, so small and ill-equipped, make little impact on our daily lives. Even the reserve units that once furnished a core of community life have shrunk into irrelevance. In schools and universities, few teach our military past. In an age of selfishness, it has become fashionable to sneer at those who risked everything for a country or a cause.

Will Canadians remember how other, older Canadians helped win the most important war of our century? Not if we don't help them. The Normandy campaign of 1944 ranks among the most decisive battles of the twentieth century and perhaps of our civilization. Stalin's evil regime might have defeated Hitler's Nazi empire, but liberal and social democracy in Europe would have vanished as they did throughout the Soviet Union. The terrible gamble of landing on an open and defended shore had to be risked. Allied soldiers fought and died in the fields of Normandy so that liberty and justice could prevail.

A hundred thousand Canadians shared three months of savage fighting. Canadian sailors delivered Canadian soldiers to Juno beach. Canadian airmen bested Hitler's Luftwaffe and battered his armoured divisions. Canadians from every part of Canada fought the finest soldiers in Europe, from the beaches in front of Bernières-sur-Mer to the desperate final struggle at St. Lambert-sur-Dives. Sometimes they lost; always they came back to try again and, finally, to win.

The history of the Normandy campaign has often been written but even the best of such books usually ignores the Canadian divisions, lumping them with the British, sometimes condemning them for their "slowness" and then revealing, in a few frail references, the limits of their research. Colonel Charles Stacey's official history, magisterial in its scope, thorough in its command of Allied and German sources, restrained in its judgements, remains largely unread.

Since 1980, more Canadians have taken a hand, armed with hindsight and eager to praise and to blame. Serving officers like Colonel Jack English have asked legitimate questions about the lessons their generation can learn from the training, equipment and leadership of the Canadians in Normandy. In *The Valour and the Horror*, a controversial television program, Brian and Terence McKenna revealed how easy battlefield decisions always are for those who have never had to make them. Still others have complained that Canadian colonels and generals lacked the ruthlessness of their German counterparts or, alternatively, that they should have let their allies do more of the fighting and dying.

This is not that kind of book. It is not a training manual for some future battle. Nor is it a tract against war. Both authors know that almost everything good in our lives and those of our families depended on the sacrifices made by young men half a century ago in Normandy. When we came to understand the Normandy campaign better, we came to an added respect and admiration for those who did their best in the hideously alien environment of war. We came to record and to judge; we stayed to comprehend. We have written this book to share our understanding of their ordeal and their accomplishments in that hot summer of 1944.

We want Canadians to know that the old men we call veterans were then as young as nineteen or twenty. When they went out to battle, they faced an enemy that was better led, trained and armed. These Canadians feared death, but they wanted to do their part. Over 5,000 of them never returned. Another 18,000 suffered wounds of mind or body that transformed or shortened their lives. None who survived the Normandy campaign was unaffected by it.

Fifty years later, remembering is the least of the obligations we owe them.

J.L. Granatstein
Desmond Morton
1994

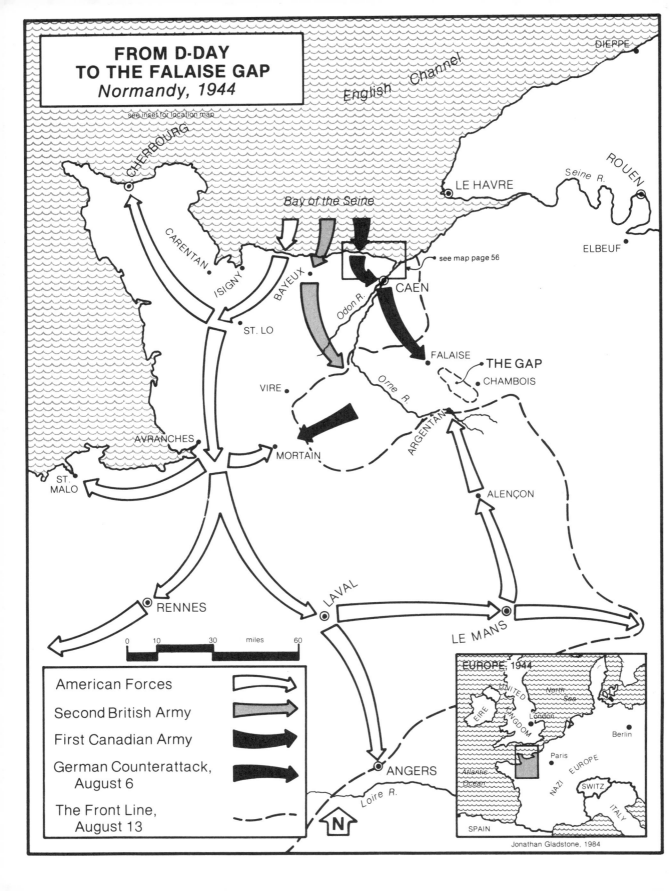

FROM D-DAY
TO THE FALAISE GAP
Normandy, 1944

see inset for location map

English Channel

DIEPPE

ROUEN

Seine R.

LE HAVRE

ELBEUF

Bay of the Seine

CHERBOURG

CARENTAN

ISIGNY

BAYEUX

Odon R.

CAEN

see map page 56

FALAISE

THE GAP

CHAMBOIS

ST. LO

VIRE

Orne R.

ARGENTAN

AVRANCHES

MORTAIN

ST. MALO

ALENÇON

RENNES

LAVAL

LE MANS

0   10   30   miles   60

ANGERS

Loire R.

American Forces

Second British Army

First Canadian Army

German Counterattack,
August 6

The Front Line,
August 13

N

EUROPE 1944

UNITED KINGDOM

EIRE

London

North Sea

Berlin

Paris

NAZI EUROPE

Atlantic Ocean

SWITZ

SPAIN

ITALY

Jonathan Gladstone, 1984

I
Prelude
to Invasion

It had been a massacre that day of August 19, 1942. The Canadians had scrambled from their ungainly landing craft directly into a storm of fire from the German positions dominating the beaches of Dieppe. There had been almost no preliminary naval bombardment to support the attackers nor much preliminary bombing to soften the defences. The Churchill tanks, struggling ashore with enormous difficulty, had found that their treads could not get purchase on the stony shingle. The 27 tanks that made it out of the water could fire their guns but, unable to move well, they could offer only limited fire support to the infantry. Worse was to come as military commanders, offshore and insulated from the chaos by faulty communications and the heavy smoke of battle, reinforced failure, sending new battalions from the floating reserve to be cut to pieces on the beaches.

A disaster to Canadian arms and Allied hopes. The Canadians of the 2nd Division had absorbed 68% casualties—3367 out of an attacking force of 4963 officers and men. 907 were killed on the beaches or died in captivity, 586 were wounded, and 1946, including many of the wounded, were taken prisoner by the victorious Germans. The defences of Fortress Europe had been tested in the largest European landing operation since Britain had been driven from the continent at Dunkirk—and the defences had proved unbreachable. In England, nervous war planners knew that the Allies had suffered a serious beating. Seizing a fortified port, seemingly a requirement for a successful invasion, had become the most difficult of tasks.

In Canada, the news of the Dieppe raid was initially reported as a triumph of initiative and dash but, as the terrible casualty lists appeared in the newspapers, there were tears in Windsor, Hamilton, Toronto, Montreal, Calgary, Ottawa, and in the prairie towns of Saskatchewan. Units had been decimated and proud regiments virtually wiped out. The Essex Scottish, the Royal Regiment of Canada, the Royal Hamilton Light Infantry, the Queen's Own Cameron Highlanders, the South Saskatchewan Regiment, the Calgary Regiment and Les Fusiliers Mont-Royal were no more—until they could be reconstituted out of survivors and replacements. The dead could never be restored; the lives of the wounded, and of the families left behind in Canada, could never be remade.

BUILDING A FIGHTING FORCE

The Canadian soldiers of the 2nd Division, like their counterparts in the Royal Canadian Navy and the Royal Canadian Air Force, had joined up voluntarily in response to their country's call to wage war against Nazi Germany. Most had never had anything to do with the armed forces before. Many were not politically sophisticated and probably largely unaware of the full dimensions of Hitlerism when they came to the recruiting office. Some had enlisted only because the army promised "three squares a day", a major consideration after years of unemployment during the Depression; some had joined up to escape domesticity and others had put on a uniform for adventure, a change, a chance to see the world. But before long, and in response to a campaign of education run by the armed forces and civilian agencies, many Canadians in and out of uniform began to realize what they were fighting for and what they were fighting against. Hitler's Germany was an unmitigated evil, and the Second World War was a just war. Many Canadians believed deeply in the worth of their cause.

At the same time, they could serve and fight without necessarily admiring everything about their own country or its leadership. The Great Depression of the 1930s had seen hundreds of thousands of young men condemned to ride the rods across the land in search of work, all too often only to end up in a relief camp administered by the Department of National Defence, usually in some out-of-the-way—and out-of-sight—location. The country had let down its citizens, and the political leadership lent no inspiration. The Conservative Prime Minister R.B. Bennett, in power from 1930 to 1935, had used bluster in a vain effort to deal with unemployment and poverty; Mackenzie King, Liberal party leader and Prime Minister from 1935 through to the end of the Second World War and beyond, had relied primarily on time to cure all ills.

Time—and the coming of the war—did resolve some of the problems. The war pushed Canada's economy into a boom, producing unlimited markets for Canadian goods and agricultural products, and servicemen overseas knew that their families at home were at least able to work and save. However, as volunteers, they felt a deep contempt for King's government and its unwillingness to impose compulsory military service in the face of Quebec's resistance. There had been bitter controversies in 1917 and 1918, when the Union Government of the First World War had imposed conscription, and King had pledged no conscription for overseas service, so the question was a delicate one. But that was a politician's problem, not a soldier's, and the men in the forces were scornful of the home defence conscripts who had been enrolled, as a political compromise, under the National Resources Mobilization Act for service in Canada. The bloody politicians and their bloody games!

The Army, anxious for combat, resented the way the government handled national questions involving the forces. The RCAF, a huge force that at its peak numbered 232,632 men and 17,030 officers, had few exclusively Canadian squadrons overseas. Most of its aircrew members were integrated in Royal Air Force squadrons and wings manned by representatives from all the Dominions, many of the British colonies, and even the conquered nations of Europe. Politicians in Ottawa worried that Canada would never receive its proper share of the credit; but the pilots, bombardiers, air gunners, navigators and wireless operators wanted to fly and were happy enough to do so with anyone, Brit, Aussie or Rhodesian, who was competent. They had the same response to the politicians' desire to keep the Canadian Army in Britain intact and not split it into penny-packets for operations. This was just Mackenzie King again, they felt, hoping against hope to prevent any need for conscription by keeping the army out of the fighting as long as possible. There was an element of truth in that—but not much. The real force against splitting the Army was General A.G.L. McNaughton, the Canadian commander in Britain.

Andy McNaughton was the soldiers' *beau idéal*—"Men loved Andy McNaughton," one remembered—and if Andy wanted to keep the Army together that was probably enough to end the argument for most of them. A scientific soldier, McNaughton possessed a magnetic personality and a palpable charm; he showed the troops that he was on their side, that he understood their needs, that he cared. Unfortunately, the British generals with whom the Canadian commander had to work and deal on a daily basis found McNaughton difficult, prickly and nationalistic, and they worried too about his ability to command a modern army in the field. "I have had to get rid of Andy McNaughton," General Sir Alan Brooke, the Chief of the Imperial General Staff, wrote in his diary. By the end of 1943 Andy was gone, sent back to Canada on sick leave.

By then, the General had lost his great fight to keep the Army together. In July 1943 the 1st Canadian Division had been sent to Sicily to play a useful part in the Allied invasion of southern Europe—the first since Dieppe to succeed. Under

General Guy Simonds, the Division had fought well in extremely difficult country, its men and tanks overcoming the mountainous terrain and winding roads as successfully as they fought the Wehrmacht, the German Army. By Ottawa's choice they stayed on to join in the assault on the Italian mainland, and the 1st Division was reinforced by the 5th Armoured Division, to become the I Canadian Corps.

Thus by March 1944, Canadian soldiers were serving in two theatres of war. In England, the First Canadian Army, a substantial formation under the command of General H.D.G. Crerar, consisted of the 2nd and 3rd Infantry Divisions, the 4th Armoured Division, and a vast array of supporting units. Eventually it would command British, Polish, Dutch, Czech and Belgian units as well. In Italy, the I Canadian Corps included the 1st Division, the 5th Armoured Division and 1st Armoured Brigade, as well as corps troops. In Canada, there were thousands of troops in training or working their way through the long and sometimes clogged pipeline to England and Italy. And there remained the more than 60,000 soldiers enrolled under the NRMA, the home defence conscription act.

It was Harry Crerar's army that would take part in the Allied invasion of Normandy. Born in 1888, Crerar was a professional soldier and, like many of the senior commanders in the Canadian Army, a graduate of the Royal Military College at Kingston, a veteran of the First World War and of Permanent Force soldiering in the 1920s and 1930s. Unlike McNaughton, his predecessor, he had no charisma, no knack for inspiring men. His forte was careful planning and caution with his men's lives, not strategic or tactical brilliance. He was, however, like McNaughton, conscious of the fact that he was responsible to the Canadian government for his men.

And the Army he led? By 1944, some of the Canadians had been in training for almost five years and had yet to hear a shot. For years they had practised war: there were battle schools, close combat courses, field exercises with and without troops for officers and men, and a myriad of technical and specialized courses. Close bonds of friendship existed within every unit, a vital element of regimental *esprit* and combat efficiency. The troops then were ready and generally well trained—at least, as well trained as the methods in use in the Canadian and British armies could make them. But too much training had bred a make-believe mood. As reluctant amateurs, many Canadian soldiers had found it hard to take "exercises" seriously. In the days to come, that would hurt.

Experienced soldiers were well aware that the only effective training for combat was that received on the battlefield itself—and except for those who had been at Dieppe, and a sprinkling of officers and men who had served with the British or with the divisions in Sicily or Italy, almost none of the Canadians had experienced actual fighting. That was a concern. So too was the magnitude of the task awaiting them. To invade Fortress Europe, to stage an operation with the potential to become an immensely greater and more terrible repetition of Dieppe, was enough to frighten everyone.

INVASION PLANNING

The problem of how to invade Europe had been a subject of military study since the defeats of 1940, but the British planners in London recognized that as long as the British Commonwealth stood alone against Hitler the likelihood of such an invasion was slim. Throughout 1941 the situation altered markedly. The Soviet Union was brought into the war by Hitler's onslaught on June 22, 1941, and on December 7 Japan attacked the American, British and Dutch possessions in the Far East. A few days later, Germany declared war on the United States. The Americans were at last in the war, and though the first few months of the world war were disastrous to Allied arms, eventual victory was becoming, if not a certainty, at least a strong probability.

Even before the Americans entered the war, secret meetings between the British and American Chiefs of Staff, sanctioned by Prime Minister Winston Churchill and President Franklin Roosevelt, had produced agreement that, in the event of American entry, the major effort would be devoted to the defeat of Germany first; only then would the full power of the Allies be turned against Japan. That decision was confirmed at the Arcadia Conference that brought the military leaders of the two allies together in Washington in December 1941. But few generals as yet were thinking of an invasion of the continent.

One of the few was Chief of the War Plans Division of the United States Army. This officer had convinced himself that the key for the Allies was to strike at Germany through offensive operations in Central Europe, to go after the vitals of Hitler's Third Reich while Russia, though battered by the German Army, still hung on in the war. By late March 1942, after consultations with, among others, General McNaughton—"he believes in attacking Europe. Thank God!" the American wrote in his diary—he had produced his scheme for the Chief of Staff, General George C. Marshall. As amended and refined, the plan, codenamed Roundup, called for an invasion of France by April 1, 1943 with 30 American and 18 British divisions (the latter figure presumably including the Canadians), to be landed somewhere between Le Havre and Boulogne with a view to an advance on Antwerp. The planner was Brigadier-General Dwight D. Eisenhower.

After long and contentious discussions in London between Marshall and the British Chiefs, there was agreement. Roundup would go forward in 1943, although the British had serious concerns about the transport situation—7000 landing craft would be required, almost none of which had been built—and about Japanese threats to India. Until then, the only moves against the continent would be raids. That decision led to the attack on Dieppe in 1942—a disaster that gave everyone pause.

The main lessons of Dieppe were that it was extremely dangerous to attempt to seize a defended port, and that massive preliminary bombardment—not the puny fire of a few destroyers—was essential if the invading force was to get ashore successfully. This meant intense naval and air bombardment; it meant finding a way to employ the firepower of the invading army while it was still on the landing craft; and it meant the development of special vessels, such as the Landing Craft Tank (Rocket), to drench the beaches with explosives. Another problem revealed by Dieppe, poor communication with the beaches, led to heavy investment in improved wireless equipment.

The invasion of Sicily in 1943 gave the planners a chance to test the new landing craft that were now coming off the lines. The Landing Ship Tank (LST) had entered production, a ship capable of putting as many as twenty tanks directly on the beach if the gradient was modest. The Landing Craft Infantry (LCI) could carry 200 infantry ashore, the Landing Craft Assault (LCA) about 25, and the amphibious vehicle known as the DUKW could carry men and supplies from ship to shore and inland. Special armoured equipment was also being produced or planned—swimming tanks, tanks with flails to explode mines, tanks with flamethrowers, and even tanks to fill ditches with large bundles, called fascines. There were also Assault Vehicles, Royal Engineers, or AVREs, with short-range guns firing huge explosives. The organization necessary to permit offloading of the immense tonnage of supplies modern armies consumed each day was also being worked out, and the use of undefended beaches was allowed for, a necessity if the capture of a port by frontal assault was anticipated to be costly. The implements and tactics of D-Day, as the invasion was now called, were beginning to come together.

Planning for the invasion of France was under the direction of Lieutenant-General F.E. Morgan, the Chief of Staff to the Supreme Allied Commander (Designate) or COSSAC. A British officer, Morgan had been appointed to his post in March 1943—before a Supreme Commander had been decided. That the appointment came as late as it did effectively killed Eisenhower's plan for an invasion in 1943; the Sicily campaign and the later assault on Italy meant that there would not be enough landing craft available in any case.

COSSAC's planning target date was now May 1, 1944 and Morgan's staff, largely British and American but including a few Canadians, set to work. The forces assigned to the attack were to be 5 infantry divisions "simultaneously loaded in landing craft", 2 more for follow-up purposes, 2 airborne divisions, and a further 20 divisions to be used for build-up purposes. Unfortunately, there seemed to be no prospect of acquiring sufficient landing craft to carry 5 divisions at once—"the destinies of two great empires," Winston Churchill groaned, "seem to be tied up on some god-damned things called LSTs"—and the planning had to be based on a three-division assault.

Where should the attack fall? To select a suitable site was a complex process involving port and beach capacities, naval and air facilities accessible to the enemy and eventually to the invaders, and the availability of Allied forces. The need for air cover limited the area of choice drastically, making a landing possible only between Cherbourg in France and Flushing in Belgium; the suitability of the beaches limited the choice further to either the Pas de Calais or the Cotentin-Caen area. The Pas de Calais had much to recommend it—it was only twenty miles across the English Channel and the beaches were almost ideal. But the Germans were quite capable of drawing similar conclusions. The Cotentin-Caen area had drawbacks—it was a greater distance by sea and air, increasing turn-around time. However, the beach defences were relatively light, and the beaches themselves were acceptable. The choice, therefore, was Cotentin-Caen, the Normandy coast.

The operation was undeniably a risky one. Three divisions, perhaps 30,000 fighting soldiers, were not much to hurl across a defended shore. General Morgan insisted that three conditions had to be met before Overlord, as the invasion was codenamed, could go ahead. German fighter aircraft had to be reduced in number through a major Allied air offensive. The Wehrmacht reserves in France and the Low Countries could be no more than 12 first-class divisions, excluding coastal defence and training formations, and the German High Command could not be in a position to transfer troops from the Eastern Front within the first days of D-Day or move reserves against the bridgehead at a rate exceeding 3 divisions on D-Day or 9 divisions by D-Day-plus-8. Finally, a method had to be found of providing an artificial port so supplies could get ashore.

Morgan's outline was submitted to the Combined Chiefs of Staff at their conference at Quebec City in August 1943 and endorsed. Detailed planning was now authorized and at the end of 1943 the Supreme Allied Commander, General Dwight D. Eisenhower, was named by President Roosevelt. In less than three years, Eisenhower had risen from comparatively junior rank to the most important post in the Allied armies. But because an American was supreme commander, British pride—and the British contribution to the projected assault—required that a British officer command the armies in Normandy. Eisenhower's preferred candidate was General Sir Harold Alexander, but Prime Minister Churchill and the Chief of the Imperial General Staff opted instead for General Sir Bernard Montgomery, the victor of El Alamein and the most charismatic British soldier of the war. British officers would also head the air and sea elements of the invasion.

Both Montgomery and Eisenhower—already popularly known as Monty and Ike—found immediate fault with COSSAC's Overlord plan: the front was too narrow and the 3-division assault too weak. As a result, Montgomery and his air and sea commanders reworked the plan, now called Neptune in its assault phase, into one projecting landings by the First United States Army on the right and the Second British Army on the left. A total of 5 British and Canadian infantry brigades and 3 American regimental combat teams would land in the initial assault—in effect, a 5-division front spread over fifty miles; as well, 2 airborne divisions would drop on the American flank in the pre-dawn hours, and 1 on the British and Canadian. By the evening of D-Day, the Allies expected to have 8 infantry divisions and 14 armoured regiments ashore. Finally, the date was delayed one month, a necessity in light of the landing craft situation and the increased size of the invading force.

By May 8, 1944, General Eisenhower had fixed dawn on June 5 as the best date for the attack. The tides were such that if the weather was bad that day, the plan could be mounted successfully on June 6 or 7, but thereafter a long delay would ensue before tidal conditions again permitted the invasion. The invasion date and location was one of the most closely held secrets of the war. (Secrecy was breached when a drunken Canadian brigadier shouted out the details in public. Although many must have heard, the listeners' security consciousness was such that the information did not fall into German hands.) At long last, almost four years after Dunkirk and two years after Dieppe, the Allies were ready to return to France to fight the Germans.

THE ENEMY

The German Army in 1944 was not as effective and efficient as it had been four years before. Three years of gruelling war against the Soviet Union in the East had resulted in casualties in the millions—1.7 million in the year from November 1942 to October 1943, for example—the destruction of leadership cadres and the loss of huge quantities of equipment. The Anglo-American victories in North Africa and Sicily, too, as well as the enormous weight of *matériel* that the Allies could bring to bear on the Third Reich, had all contributed to a decline in morale and battle strength. But if Germany was weaker than it had been, there was no doubt that the Wehrmacht remained the best fighting force anywhere. "They had been raised and trained to fight," one leading British military historian noted. "They were also accustomed to victory, even against apparently overwhelming odds. Their leaders and soldiers were confident that they would deal as competently with the Americans and British as they had consistently done with the Russians." Although new and improved weaponry gave the Germans added firepower and superb tanks, the strength of the German army lay in its junior leaders, men with the great talent of motivating their new recruits.

This was true even in France where the Wehrmacht had only several first-class units. After the Russian campaign had begun in June 1941, France and the Low Countries served primarily as a training area where new divisions were formed, brought to strength and, when judged battle-ready, shipped to the charnel-house in the East. The depleted units then returned to France for refitting and rebuilding. As a result, by late 1943 there were few battle-ready units among the 856,000 men of the German Army in France, particularly along the coast.

The coastal defences were primarily in the hands of static units, divisions without effective transport except for a smattering of trucks and horse-drawn wagons. Because these divisions had repeatedly been stripped of their best men for service in the East, the troops that remained tended to be a motley lot—the very young or the very old, frost-bitten veterans from the Russian Front, or members of *Ostbataillone,* units formed of captured Soviet POWs or sometimes of Polish conscripts. The loyalty and fighting ability of the 60,000 Russians was dubious. Even the purely German units on the coast, with soldiers averaging thirty-seven years of age, were not expected to do anything more than absorb the first shock of the Allied invasion.

How then was France to be defended? The Commander-in-Chief in the West, Field-Marshal Gerd von Rundstedt, a skilled professional who understood his situation very clearly, realized that the coast could never provide an unbreachable shell. His defence plan, therefore, had to be based on mobile panzer reserves—armoured and motorized divisions—that would strike from their inland bases at the Allied bridgeheads as soon as possible after the landing. Rundstedt's analysis won the Führer's support, and in November 1943 Hitler issued a decree that called for the build-up of the defences in the West:

> The hard and costly struggle against Bolshevism during the last two and a half years has demanded extreme exertions.... But the situation has since changed...a greater danger now appears in the west; an Anglo-Saxon landing. In the east, the vast extent of territory makes it possible for us to lose ground...without a fatal blow.... It is very different in the west. Should the enemy succeed in breaching our defences on a wide front here, the immediate

consequences would be unpredictable.... I can, therefore, no longer take responsibility for further weakening in the west, in favour of other theatres of war. I have therefore decided to reinforce its defences....

As a result, from the end of 1943 Wehrmacht strength in France increased. By D-Day there were 10 panzer or panzer-grenadier (armoured infantry) divisions in place, of which 6 were battle-ready.

Equally important, Hitler had decided to put Field-Marshal Erwin Rommel, perhaps the only German officer who had won as much adulation in the West as in his own country, in charge of the defences in the West. Rommel had seen his Afrika Korps destroyed by Allied air attacks, and he was afraid that if the German plan in France was based on the movement of major armoured forces, Allied air superiority would make defence impossible. It was his judgement that the Atlantic Wall had to be strengthened and the reserves located as close to the coast as possible, a position which brought him into conflict with von Rundstedt. In the end, Hitler produced a weak compromise that left each field-marshal in charge of some panzer divisions, although there was no doubt that the Führer favoured a fight on the beaches. In March 1944, Hitler told his generals that if the Allies could be crushed there, "the enemy will never try to invade again....they would need months to organize a fresh attempt. And an invasion failure would also deliver a crushing blow to British and American morale...."

Rommel's strengthening of the Atlantic Wall began in earnest early in 1944. His plans called for laying millions of mines on land and the construction of tetrahedra obstacles—three iron bars intersecting at right angles—on the beaches, as well as planting mines and interconnected stakes on suitable landing-grounds inland. By D-Day the work was well under way—over four million mines had been laid, for example—but fortunately for the Allies it was far from complete. Although Rommel had written on May 5 that he was "more confident than ever before. If the British give us just two more weeks, I won't have any more doubt about it," in fact there was little defence in depth and supplies for the construction of obstacles remained hard to secure. To add to the problem, the high-quality divisions in France continued to be rushed to the East to meet emergencies. The 9th and 10th SS Panzer Divisions had been pulled out in March, the Panzer Lehr Division was shipped to Hungary and did not return until May, and the efficient Hermann Göring SS Panzer Division, promised to France, was tied up in Italy. Nonetheless, within striking distance of the coast the Germans still had five first-class divisions: the 12th SS Panzer Division, made up of fanatical *Hitlerjugend* (Hitler Youth), fifty miles behind the coast; the Panzer Lehr

Division in the Le Mans area; the 21st Panzer Division, under Rommel's direct control, in the Caen area; and 2 more tank divisions north of the Seine. In addition, the Wehrmacht deployed 32 static divisions, of widely varying quality, along the French and Dutch coasts.

Along the Norman coast, the area crucial to the Allies, the Germans had positioned the 243rd, the 709th, the 352nd, and the 716th Infantry Divisions, all of which (except for the 352nd, which had only recently been posted to Normandy in response to one of Hitler's intuitive flashes) were static formations. The D-Day invasion would fall mainly on the 352nd and the 716th, Juno Beach, the beach where the Canadians were to land, being held by the latter division. Its strength on May 1 was 7771 all ranks, including two *Ostbataillone*. The division, one Canadian officer later noted, was made up of "third-rate troops", but because of the fortifications and Rommel's resistance nests commanding the beach the 716th was to prove stout enough behind its concrete. Rommel also had elements of the 21st Panzer Division stationed in the 716th's area, and there were 2 panzer-grenadier battalions and 1 anti-tank battalion only five miles inland.

But it was the beach defences that were of immediate concern. The resistance nests, with their massive concrete pillboxes and artillery or anti-tank weapons, surrounded by trenches with mortars or machine-guns, could both take and inflict punishment. On the three beaches where the Allies would land the Germans had mounted 25 guns, including two of the feared 88mm guns, and 11 heavy mortars. The potential for heavy casualties was there.

PREPARING FOR THE ASSAULT

Throughout the long period of training and waiting in England, the Canadians had grown accustomed to hearing themselves described as a dagger pointing at the heart of Berlin, as a spearhead force of picked assault troops. Some early exercises and indeed some planning had envisaged General McNaughton's headquarters playing a critical part, even a directing one, in the invasion and subsequent battle. American and British national sensibilities would probably have ruled out such a grandiose Canadian role—of the 23 infantry, 10 armoured and 4 airborne divisions in England by D-Day, only 3 were Canadian. Though the initial COSSAC plan did not call for a Canadian contribution in the assault, under Montgomery's revised version a place was given to one Canadian division on D-Day and the First Canadian Army was assigned to a follow-up role.

The Canadian division selected was the 3rd, commanded by Major-General R.F.L. Keller, with the 2nd Canadian Armoured Brigade also under his command.

In accord with the Neptune plan, the 3rd was to be directed by the I British Corps in the assault, and Keller's officers began to work with the Corps headquarters as early as November 1943. By February 1944, unit commanders were being briefed. The infantry training phase was intensive, involving the study and practice of amphibious assaults, of combined operations, of embarkation and disembarkation. Exercise followed exercise, dummy-run followed dummy-run, initially at Combined Training Centres in Scotland. Battalions practised landings supported by artillery firing from the landing craft—one attempt to apply a lesson learned from Dieppe—and later exercises brought brigades and eventually divisions to run through their manoeuvres.

The 2nd Armoured Brigade, intended to land with the first wave to support the infantry, also had to master the tactics of the assault. The 1st Hussars and the Fort Garry Horse, the two regiments involved in the initial phase, each received two squadrons of new Sherman tanks equipped with the ingenious DD or Duplex Drive, a gearing device that enabled the engine to operate the tracks on land, and a propeller in the water; a canvas wall around the hull displaced enough water to let the armoured vehicle float. All the other tanks and vehicles of the regiments—and indeed virtually the entire wheeled and tracked equipment of the invasion force—had to be waterproofed, and the process had to be 100 per cent thorough to permit immersion in up to four feet of water. This was a time-consuming chore, and difficult technically, particularly for the tankers who only received the Shermans in May. Moreover, the armoured regiments had to master the tactics of amphibious assault—as did the 3rd Division's artillery, re-equipped for the invasion with Priests, 105mm guns mounted in a tank chassis.

At last, towards the end of May, the Canadians, along with their British and American colleagues, began moving to concentration areas on the south coast of England. On May 26, all camps were sealed and no one could enter or leave without a special pass. (One regimental commander wrote later that he could not even visit parts of his unit without this pass.) On June 1, the first Canadian units began boarding their ships, the sequence of embarkation and the precise order in which stores were loaded having been carefully worked out well before. By June 4, everything was ready.

"The actual loading went very smoothly indeed," the Commanding Officer of the Fort Garry Horse later recalled. "We were entrucked at the marshalling camp about 2330 hours, on an hour or so warning, and moved to our tanks and vehicles...we moved off in the dark by a devious one-way route.... At dawn we arrived...took on rations, topped up [gas tanks] and embarked on our L.C.T. (4). By about 0700 hours we had backed off and with three other L.C.T. (4) moved up the SOLENT.... About noon on June 5 we guessed that the big show was approved and we cast off about 1400 hours.... It was not until we passed the boom off Portsmouth that our battle maps were issued, together with a booklet about France and a message from General Crerar. I then had a final Orders Group before too many became seasick."

The basic invasion plan called for the Allies "to secure a lodgement on the Continent from which further offensive operations can be developed." To do this, 2 U.S. divisions would land at Utah and Omaha Beaches, and 2 British divisions would land on Gold and Sword Beaches, Juno Beach being the 3rd Division's target. Several hours ahead of the landings, 3 airborne divisions would drop on the flanks. The American objective following the assault was to capture Cherbourg as soon as possible and to develop operations south towards St. Lô. The Canadians and the British were to drive the bridgehead south of the Caen–St. Lô line, to capture suitable airfield sites and to protect the Americans' flank.

To get the troops to France and to support them with firepower as they went ashore was the task of the Allied navies. Commanded by Admiral Sir Bertram Ramsay, the D-Day fleet comprised the astonishing total of 7016 vessels, including 6 battleships, 2 monitors, 22 cruisers, 93 destroyers, 71 corvettes and thousands of landing craft in amazing variety. Among this array were a substantial number of ships of the Royal Canadian Navy.

The RCN's large share in the invasion was an indication of the growth of the Navy since the outbreak of war. Canadian destroyers, minesweepers, corvettes and motor torpedo boats all played a part in the attack. Sixteen minesweepers had the delicate task of clearing and marking a series of channels from the seaward edges of the thickly sown German minefields to the beaches. The work was exacting and it had to be done well; otherwise the heavily laden ships, and ultimately the success of the operation, could be jeopardized. HMCS *Prince Henry* and *Prince David*, 2 armed merchant cruisers converted into landing ships, carried 14 landing craft between them. Three RCN flotillas of landing craft also participated. In all, 110 ships of the RCN and 10,000 Canadian sailors were present at the launching of the Second Front.

The invasion fleet was covered by a huge air umbrella involving 171 squadrons of fighters and fighter bombers, ready to beat off the Luftwaffe or to attack ground positions. The road to D-Day had already been paved by a massive and co-ordinated campaign of bombing. In addition to air attacks on Germany itself, a campaign that was reducing Germany to rubble though it cost the lives of many bomber crews, the Allies struck hard at the communications networks in France.

The railway system was shattered. Traffic dropped by almost one third. Bridges over the Seine and the Loire were knocked down, virtually isolating Normandy. The Luftwaffe's radar network was wiped out and its fighters were challenged at every opportunity, the planes destroyed in the air and on the ground and pilots lost in large numbers. And because the Germans might have been able to guess the location of the pending invasion from a study of the air targets, the Allied commanders devised a deception plan designed to persuade the Germans that the attack might fall on the Pas de Calais: almost every ton of bombs to back the Normandy landing was matched by a ton dropped on the Pas de Calais area. In the final hours before the invasion, Bomber Command of the RAF—with many of its air crew wearing Canada flashes on their shoulders—unloaded 6000 tons of bombs on German coastal batteries. At first light, the American bombers dropped 4800 tons more. "This was," one Canadian flying with 244 Squadron wrote, "by far the heaviest tonnage that I have heard predicted for one operation."

The air plan was matched by other efforts at deception. The Germans were known to have particular regard for the American general George S. Patton, so Patton's headquarters were located in East Anglia, the ideal location for an attack on the Pas de Calais; and his radio operators were deliberately more careless than they might have been. Among other units, II Canadian Corps (less the 3rd Division) moved its headquarters to Kent, thus reinforcing the illusion. Even days after the Normandy attack, the German fear that the real assault would hit the Pas de Calais kept troops tied down in static locations.

Extensive security surrounded the construction of two Mulberries, artificial harbours that overcame the difficulties of seizing a port in Normandy. Building the harbours in secret was an extraordinary feat, given the huge size of the concrete components and the tens of thousands of workers involved. From October 1943 the Kentish marshes near London had seen workers erecting the steel for huge caissons, each 200 feet long, 56 feet wide, and 60 feet high; elsewhere, pierheads, buffer pontoons and breakwaters of sunken ships were assembled. Completed soon after D-Day, the Mulberries were a brilliant answer to the Allies' need to funnel huge amounts of vehicles and supplies ashore quickly.

THE CANADIAN PLAN OF ATTACK

The attack of the Canadian 3rd Division at Juno Beach was to go in on a two-brigade front: the 7th Canadian Infantry Brigade would land on Mike sector, and the 8th on Nan. Within Mike and Nan were the villages of

Courseulles-sur-Mer, Bernières-sur-Mer and the western edges of St. Aubin-sur-Mer, and the beaches, while generally well suited to a landing, had a sea approach complicated by rocky offshore ledges. Fortunately, there were few natural hindrances to block the exit of infantry or vehicles from the beaches.

The Canadians' D-Day plan called for the infantry and armour to seize an area extending almost ten miles inland. Initial objectives, including the seaside towns, were encompassed within the line Yew and the second phase line was designated Elm. The final objective of the first day included the high ground west of Caen and was designated Oak. By the time Oak had been reached, the divisional reserve, the 9th Canadian Infantry Brigade and the tanks of the Sherbrooke Fusiliers would be ashore and in position to reinforce the rest of the division during the anticipated German counter-attack.

The infantry in the first few waves would be backed by co-ordinated air and naval bombardment. The bombing of the Juno Beach defences was to begin half an hour before the landing and last for fifteen minutes; heavy bombing would then begin on the assault flanks and last until H-Hour, the actual time of the landing. Thereafter, bombers would attack enemy headquarters and communications centres inland. The ships' fire would begin while the landing craft were heading for shore. Two cruisers would shell the German batteries that protected Juno while destroyers would hit targets on the flanks. Artillery going ashore in the landing craft would also add its weight to the naval fire.

The basic weapons for the assault, however, were those carried by the infantry: rifles, Bren guns, Sten guns, grenades and PIAT (Projector Infantry Anti-Tank weapons) when the fighting intensified, backed by the 75mm guns and machine-guns of the supporting Shermans. On Mike sector, assigned to the 7th Canadian Infantry Brigade, the Regina Rifles and the Royal Winnipeg Rifles, with one company of the Canadian Scottish attached, had the right flank of Juno, their initial objective being to overwhelm the beach defences and proceed inland. On Nan sector, assigned to the 8th Canadian Infantry Brigade, the Queen's Own Rifles had the challenge of securing the beach defences and seizing Bernières, while on their left the North Shore Regiment from New Brunswick had a similar task at St. Aubin. In reserve on Mike was the Canadian Scottish; on Nan it was Le Régiment de la Chaudière. Two and a half hours after H-Hour, the reserve brigade, the 9th, consisting of the infantry of the North Nova Scotia Highlanders, the Highland Light Infantry, and the Stormont, Dundas and Glengarry Highlanders, and the tanks of the Sherbrooke Fusiliers, were to touch down.

The plan also assigned vital roles to the 3rd Division artillery which was to land and proceed to designated gun areas. The tanks of the 1st Hussars and the

Fort Garrys were to support the 7th and 8th Brigades, their DD tanks landing ahead of the infantry and engaging beach defences in the critical first minutes. In addition, Crab tanks provided by the British army were to detonate mines, using short lengths of chain on a revolving drum in front of the vehicles. The Royal Canadian Engineers had the job of clearing away underwater obstacles on the beaches and of preparing vehicle exits. And the Royal Canadian Corps of Signals had to ensure that the commanders at all levels knew what was happening over their radios and, as soon as they could be laid, over telephone lines. Not long after the initial landings, service and support troops were to come ashore, their trucks and specialized vehicles carrying the food, ammunition, oil and gas the army needed to survive. It was a co-ordinated plan, a careful plan but, as with every operation, no one could predict how the enemy might react.

The day after the Dieppe raid, a German plane kindly dropped pictures like this one to remind Canadians that Europe was impregnable. The Churchill tanks left on the beach had thick armour but a tiny gun and a feeble engine. In any case, it was almost impossible for them to get over the sea-wall and into the town. The Allies were determined not to repeat such mistakes on D-Day. (C29866/Public Archives Canada)

William Lyon Mackenzie King chats with a future Tory opponent, Major-General George Pearkes, a Victoria Cross winner in the earlier war. Though most soldiers overseas thought King was a weak and even embarrassing war-time leader and did not recognize his difficulties in keeping Canada united behind the war effort, oddly enough they would support King's postwar program of social reform. (PA132774/Public Archives Canada)

General A.G.L. McNaughton was the architect of the Canadian army in England during the early years of the war. A strong nationalist, popular with his men and a "scientific" soldier, McNaughton raised doubts among British generals about his ability to command troops in battle. (PA132648/Public Archives Canada)

Winston Churchill and General Dwight D. Eisenhower—a military-minded politician and a politically astute general—were to have second thoughts about their field commander, General Montgomery. Neither of them really understood Monty's strategy, and both would try to meddle at crucial moments in the campaign. (Imperial War Museum)

Mackenzie King wanted Canadians to believe that he was an equal of Winston Churchill and Franklin Delano Roosevelt in managing the war, but he had too much sense to butt in when Roosevelt and Churchill made decisions. The Normandy landings were decided at Quebec, where Canada provided the whisky and most of the photographers. (C4250/Public Archives Canada)

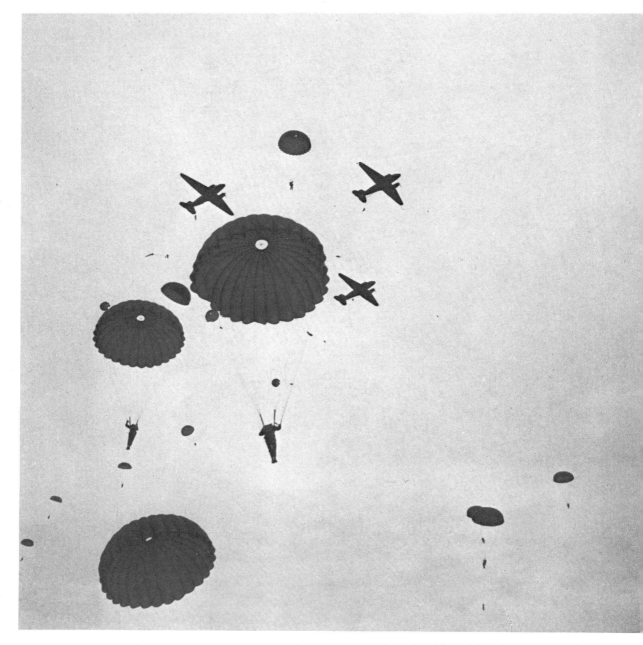

Airborne divisions were intended to protect the Allied beachhead from a quick German counter-attack. Units like the 1st Canadian Parachute Battalion were among the elite of the army, but their fighting value was limited by the difficulties of regrouping on the ground and by severe limits on the weapons and ammunition they could carry. Raw courage and light weapons were not much use against heavy tanks. (PA132785/Public Archives Canada)

For years, Canadian troops prepared themselves for battle while staff officers, with experience of the First World War (or no war at all), dreamed up ways to keep them busy. Obstacle courses like this one were supposed to test leadership and courage. They may have contributed to the unreality. Certainly no Canadian in action ever played this kind of game. (PA132776/Public Archives Canada)

Achetez des OBLIGATIONS de la VICTOIRE

**SPARTAN EXERCISES
— U. K. —**

**"RIGHT NOW ME OLE DOGS ARE SO TIRED
THEY'RE WALKIN' FROM MEMORY!"**

"Herbie", the creation of Bing Coughlin and James Douglas MacFarlane, lived
a cartoonist's version of a Canadian soldier's hopes and fears. Herbie had lost
his illusions—he was determined to survive sergeants, officers, the Provost
Corps and even the Germans. Coughlin was a feature cartoonist in the Canadian Army's paper, *The Maple Leaf.* (Bing Coughlin, *Herbie* (Toronto: 1946) p. 11;
reproduced by permission of the Minister of Supply and Services Canada.)

OPPOSITE: Total war was financed by heavy wartime taxes and by borrowing
excess spending-power from Canadians, who were earning more than most
had dreamed possible in the dreary Depression years. French Canadians, like
English Canadians, were urged to back their fighting men with Victory Bonds.
(PA72-5036/Public Archives Canada)

OVERLEAF: Historians often portray Montgomery as a cautious general with an
excessively prickly ego. He also had a flair for publicity and a shrewd awareness that, in a democratic army, soldiers must know and trust their generals.
One way to beat Rommel's mystique was to show Montgomery's troops that
their general was every bit as sharp. Each inspection trip ended like this, with
soldiers crowded around to hear Montgomery for themselves. Canadians might
resent the clipped British accent and obvious self-importance but Monty was a
bright contrast to their own rather colourless commanders. (PA132891/Public
Archives Canada)

A Landing Craft (Assault) carried about a platoon of infantry. Its crew had a
little protection from rifle bullets, but once the ramp was down the troops
would be on their own. Wading ashore on a smooth English beach was a pale
preparation for the real thing. (PA131548/Public Archives Canada)

Landing Craft (Infantry) carried a whole company ashore, pouring them down twin gangways while a light gun in the bow tackled any opposition. These Canadians, already equipped with their new "D-Day" helmets, wait to land on a beach off the south of England only a month before D-Day. (PA132929/ Public Archives Canada)

OVERLEAF: A company of the Highland Light Infantry of Canada board the LCI while relaxed Canadian seamen watch the heavy-laden "pongos" and speculate on their chances. One of the innumerable D-Day preparations was laying acres of prefab paving on English beaches so that loading like this would be faster and safer. (PA132811/Public Archives Canada)

A few days before D-Day officers of the Fort Garry Horse gathered outside brigade headquarters "somewhere in England" for a final photograph. Soon, 9 of these officers would be dead and 16 more would be wounded; only 10 survived unscathed. For a Canadian armoured regiment in the Normandy campaign, it was not an especially heavy toll. (Author's collection)

Men of the Highland Light Infantry of Canada perform the oldest army drill—
waiting. They belong to the second wave of the invasion force; their folding
bicycles are supposed to help wheel them through to Caen. Now they wait,
catch a quick smoke and watch a big Landing Ship Tank load its cargo of trucks
for a Royal Canadian Electrical and Mechanical Engineers workshop.
(PA132812/Public Archives Canada)

By June of 1944, ports all over the south of England were as jammed as this dock at Southampton. Only complete Allied air superiority made scenes like this possible: if the Luftwaffe had ever got through, the camouflage nets over

the boatloads of tanks and trucks would have fooled no one. The concentration of men and equipment in southern England helped spread the joke that the island would have a permanent tilt. (PA132653/Public Archives Canada)

HMCS *Prince David* was a former Canadian passenger ship converted first into a cruiser for the Royal Canadian Navy and then into a mother ship for landing craft. She and her sister ship, the *Prince Robert,* were two of the best known of Canada's warships, in the Mediterranean and then off Normandy. Her little assault craft delivered American, French and British troops as well as Canadians. (PA132797/Public Archives Canada)

Lieutenant John Beveridge of the Royal Canadian Naval Volunteer Reserve plays cribbage with one of his crew as their landing craft waits for an exercise to continue. Naval officers went ashore as beachmasters, struggling to control traffic as hosts of landing craft jostled for a chance to land and clear off—hence Beveridge's pistol and the Commando badge on his shoulder. (PA132794/Public Archives Canada)

Once aboard and carefully sealed off, so that loose lips wouldn't sink ships, the troops were briefed. Captain S. Mendelsohn from Montreal goes through the motions with a self-conscious flock of soldiers to please the photographer, but his map is not of Normandy. The troops are wearing inflatable life-preservers, designed to go over their battledress and equipment. (PA132882/Public Archives Canada)

Company Sergeant-Major D.D. Perkins from Ottawa finds a comfortable spot on the front seat of his truck to write a letter home. One worry for invasion planners was that soldiers, crammed into the landing ships, would lose their "fighting edge" during the long wait for action. (PA132881/Public Archives Canada)

OVERLEAF: One reason for Germans to believe that a Normandy landing was impossible was that there were no port facilities on the long open beaches. The Allies had a top-secret answer: two "Mulberry" artificial harbours, one each for the British and the Americans. Immense concrete caissons would be floated across to France and sunk, together with obsolete warships, to form a break-water; then prefabricated piers would be fitted in place to help freighters unload. (York University — *Toronto Telegram* collection)

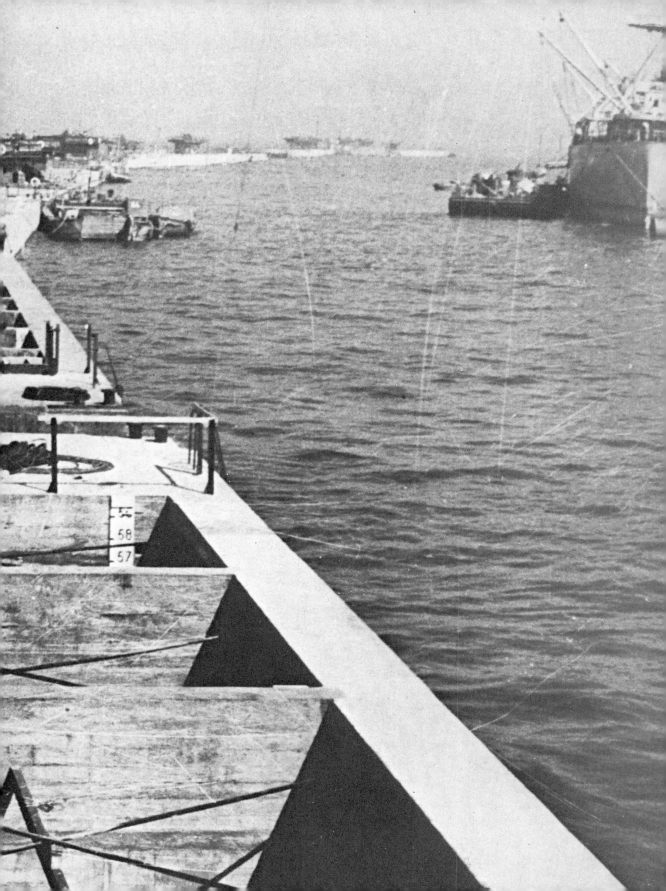

How vital a breakwater could be is evident from this oblique aerial photo of the British Mulberry. While ships wait beside the concrete caissons, others unload at the pierhead. When storms knocked out the American harbour, ton-

nages were unloaded on the open beach, using landing craft and amphibious
trucks. The British managed to keep their harbour functioning. (York
University — *Toronto Telegram* collection)

Allied planning for D-Day counted on massive and prolonged bombing of road and rail junctions in France, so that the invasion area would be isolated. To keep the Germans guessing, Allied air forces had to spread out their targets so that both Normandy and the Pas de Calais would be affected. These Lancasters, flown by the RCAF, were the finest British bombers of the war—they could carry seven tons of bombs at 210 miles an hour. (PL26185/Public Archives Canada)

Field-Marshal Erwin Rommel had captured the imagination of Germany—and of the Allies—by his brilliant defensive battles in North Africa. His mystique and his energy added to the difficulties of any Allied invasion of France. In the end, his errors helped the Allies gain a foothold. (J20577/Public Archives Canada)

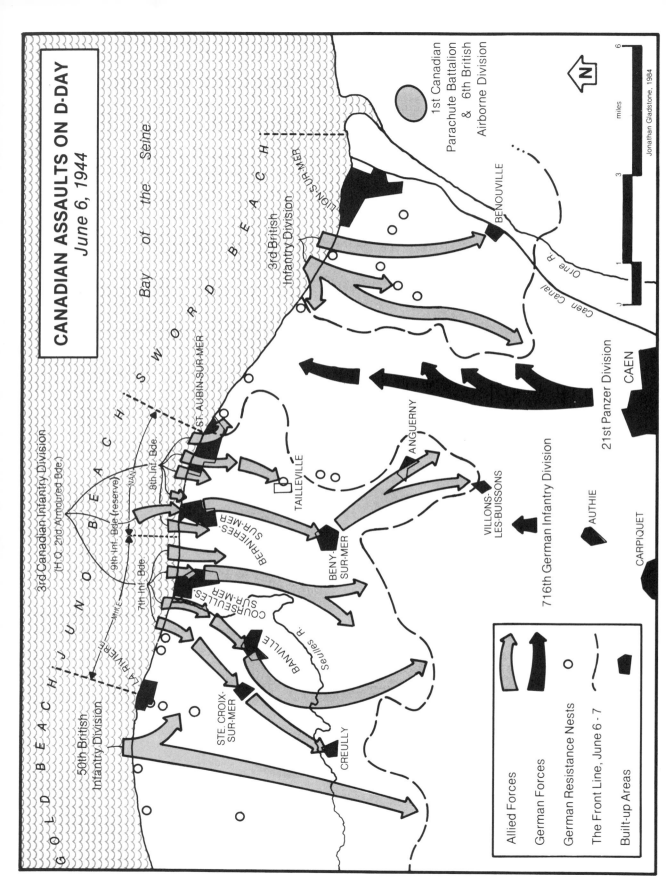

CANADIAN ASSAULTS ON D-DAY
June 6, 1944

Bay of the Seine

GOLD BEACH

JUNO BEACH

SWORD BEACH

50th British
Infantry Division

3rd Canadian Infantry Division
(H.Q. 2nd Armoured Bde.)

9th Inf. Bde. (reserve)

8th Inf. Bde.

7th Inf. Bde.

MIKE

NAN

LA RIVIERE

ST. AUBIN-SUR-MER

BERNIERES-SUR-MER

COURSEULLES-SUR-MER

STE. CROIX-SUR-MER

BANVILLE

CREULLY

TAILLEVILLE

BENY-SUR-MER

ANGUERNY

VILLONS-LES-BUISSONS

AUTHIE

CARPIQUET

Seulles R.

3rd British
Infantry Division

LION-SUR-MER

BENOUVILLE

Orne R.

Caen Canal

CAEN

21st Panzer Division

716th German Infantry Division

1st Canadian
Parachute Battalion
& 6th British
Airborne Division

Jonathan Gladstone, 1984

N

0   1   3   6
miles

Legend

Allied Forces	
German Forces	
German Resistance Nests	○
The Front Line, June 6 - 7	
Built-up Areas	

II
The Bridgehead

The first landing craft carrying the Queen's Own Rifles, a historic Toronto regiment, hit the beach at 8:12 a.m., 27 minutes later than originally planned. The sea was very rough, so rough that the DD tanks, intended to swim ashore under their own power and to arrive before the infantry, would have swamped and had to be landed from their LSTs directly on the beaches. Some that braved the five-foot waves sank like stones. Despite the minesweeping by the navy and the efforts of frogmen, there were still innumerable mines that could tear the bottom out of a landing craft, and the shore was littered with beach obstacles, most with anti-tank mines lashed to the extremities. But all the landing craft carrying the Queen's Own made it to the beach, although some suffered damage. Shaky with seasickness, the riflemen poured out of the craft and began a two-hundred-yard dash to the cover of the seawall, under a withering enemy fire.

One platoon of Major Hume Dalton's A Company came under the shelling of an 88mm gun that had not been shown on the air photographs provided before the assault. Before it could be destroyed, the gun almost wiped out the platoon — the platoon commander was wounded twice, an artillery forward observation officer was wounded, a sergeant was killed and two thirds of the men were killed or wounded. A wounded sergeant gathered the 10 or so survivors and got them to the railway station, where he collapsed. A corporal took over and led the remnant—perhaps 5 men out of the original 30—into house-clearing, ferreting out the defending Germans.

D Company, commanded by Dalton's brother Charles, ran into worse opposition. The company landed directly in front of a resistance nest that, like many that day, had survived unscathed the air and naval bombardments. Almost half the company was lost in the initial race for the seawall. Finally, after seeing comrades die in the desperate search for cover, three of the Queen's Own rose from cover and silenced the enemy nest by pitching grenades through the firing slits and using Sten guns to kill anything that moved within the concrete bunker. Lieutenant W.G. Herbert, Lance-Corporal René Tessier and Rifleman W. Chicoski had got the advance under way. Despite terrible losses, the Queen's Own Rifles of Canada were ashore and moving forward in Nan sector.

NEPTUNE SUCCEEDS

As the experiences of the Queen's Own suggest, the D-Day landings were not without their heavy casualties and mishaps. Operations Overlord and Neptune were risky undertakings at best, and the weather conditions had already forced postponement of the landings from June 5 to June 6. As it was, the seas remained high all day. Nonetheless, there can be no doubt that the invasion was a great achievement. To move 5 divisions by sea, and 3 more by air, to have more than 7000 ships approach a fortified shoreline in secrecy and to achieve both tactical and strategic surprise was an astonishing feat of arms.

Long before dawn the first attackers came from the sky: 2 American airborne divisions, the 81st and 101st, and the British 6th Airborne—including the 1st Canadian Parachute Battalion. Despite high winds from the storm that almost stopped the invasion, and navigation errors that sent many paratroopers to a watery grave, the tough airborne troops did their job—seizing key bridges and causeways inland from the invasion beaches and confusing the German defenders. The price was high. Armed with only a few light weapons and little ammunition, and often lacking communications, the paratroopers fought a score of bloody battles in the Normandy countryside throughout June 6 and for days after.

Incredibly, despite the massive air bombardment and the airborne assault, the Germans were still unprepared for what faced them on the morning of June 6. Few guns opened fire at the approaching landing craft and LSTs. The Luftwaffe flew only a tiny number of sorties against the invasion fleet—250 as opposed to more than 14,000 mounted by the Allies to cover the landings—and the German navy, weak as it was, scarcely reacted at all. A good thing, too.

Certainly there should have been opportunities to disrupt the attacks. The infantry had to pile into their tiny craft at least seven miles off the coast. Then came a rough, lurching ride through five-foot waves to the beaches. Alert defenders could have wiped out such easy targets, but the luck of most of the attackers held.

At Utah Beach on the lower part of the Cotentin peninsula, where the

American 4th Infantry Division landed, the bombing of the beach defences had generally been effective; the assault boats touched down 2000 yards south of where they should have been, a happy error that put them into a lightly defended locality. But at Omaha Beach the 1st Infantry Division, the "Big Red One", hit the sector controlled by the Wehrmacht's capable 352nd Division. The terrain was very difficult, with strong defences dominating the beaches from high ground, and the tanks had trouble reaching the shore. The Americans, having rejected the specialized armour employed by the British and Canadians, had no effective way to clear mines. The result was a bloodbath. By nightfall on D-Day, American troops had moved only 2000 yards inland. In the face of huge losses at Omaha Beach, their commanders considered that a major feat of arms.

On Gold Beach, the 50th British Division got ashore without too many problems, although German strongpoints caused casualties. Nonetheless, by nightfall Juno and Gold had linked up. On Sword the British 3rd Division, a veteran regular army formation, had landed readily enough, but the division failed to capture the Norman city of Caen, its D-Day objective, and had to fend off a weak German panzer counter-attack in the late afternoon. Still, Sword Beach was secure and the troops were well inland.

D-DAY ON JUNO

As for the Canadians on Juno, some units had an easier initiation than the Queen's Own. On the 7th Brigade's Mike sector, even though the DD tanks of the 1st Hussars ran into some difficulty getting ashore, enough made it to the beach under their own power to be in a position to give support when the Regina Rifles landed shortly after 8:00 a.m. This support was essential to a successful attack on the resistance nests of the 716th Infantry that, again, had been scarcely damaged by the bombardment.

One strongpoint, described by a Canadian war correspondent, was 35 feet across with concrete 4 feet thick. Outside the casement was a concrete-walled trench running to the water's edge and three machine-gun positions, again well protected by concrete. Behind the casement was an anti-tank gun, also in concrete and mounted on a swivel; below, underground chambers, reinforced with concrete and steel, afforded the German gun crews secure shelter. No wonder the Reginas had trouble. One 75mm gun was only wiped out when a DD tank put a shell right through its gun shield; another 88mm position was silenced by direct hits from the tanks. With this kind of fire support the Rifles were able to fight their way up from the beach and section by section began to work their way through the defended houses in Courseulles. The Regina battalion's reserve companies had widely varied experiences. C Company landed without problem, easily cleared the beaches and moved inland. D Company, however, found its landing at 8:55 a.m. disrupted when several of the assault craft hit mines concealed by the rising tide; only 49 survivors reached the beach. The Regina Rifles consolidated at the village of Reviers in late afternoon and began to push inland.

The other battalion landing at Mike sector was the Royal Winnipeg Rifles and an extra company provided by Vancouver's Canadian Scottish. The Scottish, holding the far right of the Juno front, happily found that naval gunfire had wiped out the 75mm gun commanding their beach and reached the shore without much incident. Two companies of the Winnipegs, those nearest the Scottish, met similar good fortune. But the two companies that had to clear the western edge of Courseulles faced fierce opposition. "The bombardment having failed to kill a single German," the unit war diary observed with more than a tinge of bitterness, "... these companies had to storm their positions 'cold'—and did so without hesitation." B Company came under heavy fire when its LCAs were still half a mile from the beach. Many of the Little Black Devils (as the Royal Winnipeg Rifles had been known since 1885) were hit as soon as they waded into chest-high surf. Nonetheless the battalion took the beach defences, cleared the small harbour, drove a gap through minefields—the Germans had planted 14,000 mines between Courseulles and Bernières—and liberated the small villages just off the coast. The cost was heavy. B Company was reduced from 120 men to a mere 27 by the morning's work.

The Brigade's reserve battalion, the Canadian Scottish, touched down under sporadic mortar fire at 8:30 a.m., but it took an hour for the unit to get past the beach, some of its men using bicycles brought ashore from the landing craft. By nightfall, having linked up with its company in the first wave, the Scottish had dug in around Pierrepont. The unit saw rather less action than any of the other D-Day battalions; its 87 casualties were the lightest toll paid that day by any of the infantry battalions.

On Nan sector where the Queen's Own landed, the 8th Brigade ran into stiff opposition when the high waves made it impossible to launch the DD tanks as planned. Captain C.D.A. Tweedale of the Fort Garry Horse later noted that "the waves continued to break high above the doors of the L.C.T.s" and the swim-in had to be abandoned; instead, "due to the high tide the tanks would have to launch with screens inflated within a few hundred yards of the muzzles of the beach defence guns." That was bad enough, but the LCTs failed to line up in the appropriate formation and confusion ensued. Tweedale's squadron had 4 tanks knocked out in the water, 3 of them immobilized by mines; only 13 got ashore and into action—and the tanks landed after and not before the infantry.

The North Shore Regiment found that the concrete and steel strongpoint at St. Aubin with its 100 defenders had escaped the preliminary bombardment. The New Brunswickers dealt with it, supported by Fort Garry tanks and a British AVRE. The strongpoint's 50mm anti-tank gun, however, had fired at least 70 rounds and had knocked out a number of tanks before it was destroyed. The rest of the North Shore companies, landing west of St. Aubin, had an easier time on the beach, although C Company had a six-hour battle to take Tailleville, which it managed to do by early evening with substantial assistance from the Fort Garry's Shermans. Sixty prisoners were taken in what the Fort Garry's commanding officer called a "good party". His pocket diary had the same laconic entry for each of the next three days—the single word "fighting".

The 8th Brigade's reserve battalion, Le Régiment de la Chaudière, touched down at about 8:30 a.m., also running into trouble from mines and obstacles. All but one of the LCAs carrying A Company foundered before reaching shore, and the Chaudières had to swim for it, losing much of their equipment in the process. The survivors then had to wait on the beach while the Queen's Own mopped up, prior to moving through Bernières. The inhabitants, peering cautiously out of their homes, some of which were in ruins, were astonished to discover that the Canadians were French-speaking. A CBC reporter noted that one Chaudière had replied to a question from a local by saying, "*P'tet ben que oui, p'tet ben que non,*" or "Maybe yes, maybe no." The pronunciation was almost a perfect match for that of Norman Frenchmen, and the startled soldier was kissed and told, "Look, my friend, you're not a Canadian, you're a Frenchman like me." By late afternoon, supported by the Fort Garry Horse, the battalion had moved on and taken Beny-sur-Mer. The Chaudières received timely and effective support from HMCS *Algonquin* when the Canadian destroyer dropped thirteen out of fifteen shells directly on a battery of three 88mm guns holding up the advance.

At about 11:40 a.m., landing craft of the 3rd Division's reserve brigade, the 9th, began to ride the surf into the beaches. Hundreds of infantry and dozens of tanks crowding through Bernières made all involved grateful that the Luftwaffe was staying close to its bases. It was late afternoon before the 9th Brigade was on the move towards Beny-sur-Mer. Any hope that it would seize the Carpiquet area had to be abandoned. The advance battalions of the 9th dug in around Anisy, supported by the tanks of the Sherbrooke Fusiliers.

By the end of D-Day, the Canadians were ashore and moving well inland. The German defenders had been effectively destroyed: the 716th Division reported a strength of less than one battalion out of the six that had begun the day. Almost none of the Canadian units—the sole exception was a troop of tanks of the 1st Hussars that reached Secqueville-en-Bessin—reached their Oak objectives, a result of high seas, German resistance, and the confusion and killing on the beaches. Ross Munro, a Canadian journalist, reported that "the German dead were littered over the dunes, by the gun positions. By them, lay Canadians in blood-stained battle-dress, in the sand and in the grass, on the wire and by the concrete forts. I saw friends I had known, men who had joined the army in the first months of the war—and now had died in their first action here on the Norman beach. They had lived a few minutes of this victory they had made. That was all."

The Canadians lost 340 men killed and 574 wounded on D-Day, with 47 captured. The Queen's Own suffered most, losing 143. The Winnipeg Rifles had 128 casualties; the North Shore Regiment, 125. As the Army's official historian later noted, those casualties were about half the planners had feared. But a thousand casualties is still a serious disaster, the equivalent of the elimination at a stroke of a good-sized town. D-Day was a triumph, but Canadians had paid for their success in blood.

By the night of June 8, the three British and Canadian beaches had linked up with Utah to the east. The invasion was, all told, a major Allied success. The British and Canadians had landed more than 75,000 troops and the Americans about 57,500 from the sea, and an additional 23,400 paratroops from the air. The Allies had put almost 6,000 vehicles ashore, including 900 tanks and armoured vehicles, and some 600 guns. And they had landed 4,000 tons of supplies. They were in Normandy to stay.

FIGHTING THE SS

One reason that casualties were lower than feared was the absence of a strong counter-attack. Where were the panzers? Rommel's headquarters controlled only the 21st Panzer Division near Caen. It had managed to get some tanks down to the beaches in the gap between the British and Canadian landings, although without much effect. But the major tank reserves, the 1st SS Panzer Corps situated north-west of Paris, could not be moved without the Führer's permission. All day Hitler's headquarters in remote East Prussia ignored the appeals. General Jodl, head of the military staff at the headquarters, told importunate officers on Rundstedt's staff that the Normandy invasion was only a feint to mask the real effort east of the Seine. Not until late in the afternoon of June 6 was permission granted to move the SS tanks. Once on the road, the armoured columns ran into fierce Allied air attacks. Columns of smoke marked burning German tanks and vehicles. Others waited for darkness before moving.

Hitler, a habitual late riser, did not learn of the invasion until late in the morning, General Jodl evidently preferring not to awaken his master with bad news. That was fate. So too was the fact that Field-Marshal Rommel was visiting his wife in Germany on June 6. The Army commander in Normandy was also away, running an exercise in Brittany; the panzer corps commander was visiting in Belgium; and another key officer was said to have spent the night with his mistress. The confusion in the German command was very real and much to the Allies' advantage. But the German response would not be delayed much beyond the first day.

The Canadian orders for D–Day-plus-1 were to press forward to the original D–Day objective, the Oak line. The Royal Winnipeg Rifles and the Regina Rifles headed out shortly after dawn and by noon, after very little resistance, had arrived at Oak, a distance of just over four miles. Both regiments claimed the credit for being the first Allied unit to reach their goals.

On the left of the Canadian bridgehead, General Keller's orders were for the North Nova Scotia Highlanders and the Sherbrooke Fusiliers of the 9th Brigade to begin an advance in the direction of Carpiquet and its airfield. It was a dangerous venture. During the previous night, there had been skirmishes with German troops, and prisoners had been identified as coming from the 21st Panzer Division. The Germans were ready for the Canadians. When the North Novas in their lightly armoured universal carriers and the Sherbrooke Fusiliers in their light Stuart reconnaissance tanks reached the village of Buron, they ran into well-sited German defences. What made the attackers' position even more dangerous was that their advance had outrun the range of artillery support. The result was a long and costly battle for the village by a single company of infantry and a squadron of tanks, a battle that turned into a house-by-house "search and destroy" struggle. The remainder of the column, bypassing Buron, had moved on to Authie, a mile farther south.

At Authie, Canadians faced the first major German counter-attack against the Allied bridgeheads. At the forefront was the 12th SS Panzer Division, a crack formation of *Hitlerjugend,* young soldiers raised to believe in a German master race led by an all-knowing Führer. The 12th SS also boasted tough and experienced officers and NCOs, most of them veterans of the bitter Russian campaigns. Almost two thirds of the 20,540 men of the division were 18 years of age, and the division had yet to receive its baptism of fire—except for Allied air attacks on the columns as they struggled towards the coast. The division commander reported, "I have been on my way to you for about eight hours; I lay a good four hours in roadside ditches because of air attacks." In addition, there were a battalion of tanks and three battalions of panzer-grenadiers of the 25th SS Panzer-Grenadier Regiment, commanded by *Standartenführer* (Colonel) Kurt

Meyer, the first SS soldiers to reach the battlefield. Meyer's orders were to strike to the beaches, and his first task was to recapture Buron and Authie.

By the time the panzers reached Authie, officers and men from C Company, the North Novas, had already suffered a number of casualties in the morning's fighting. As Meyer's troops closed on the village, German artillery and mortar fire began to pound the North Novas' positions. The Canadians could see the German counter-attack moving across the open fields towards them. Attempts to get artillery support or reinforcements were unavailing. By now, the German assault was also hitting Buron. The North Novas in Authie were ordered to pull back towards Buron, but few of the infantrymen managed to break contact and get away. C Company was virtually wiped out. In their first engagement, the *Hitlerjugend* were proving to be formidable foes, although the determined Nova Scotia battalion gave as good as it got. On both sides, the casualties were heavy as fighting became a brutal hand-to-hand melee. Tanks of the Sherbrooke Fusiliers churned the dust and shot plumes of black oily smoke skywards. The out-gunned Shermans with their raw crews were a poor match for Meyer's skilled command. In Authie and Buron, the Canadian defenders were overwhelmed. Many surrendered.

That evening, 23 prisoners were shot by men of the 12th SS Panzer Division. According to the account by one of the prosecutors at the subsequent war crimes trial, many of the captured Canadians had previously been wounded or disabled. Some had their hands tied behind their backs. The bodies of the murdered were left unburied and in some cases were deliberately hauled onto the roadways where they were ground into pulp by passing tanks and trucks. Most of the 23 slaughtered were Sherbrooke Fusiliers and North Novas. Later, this SS division was to commit similar atrocities against prisoners of war from the Regina Rifles, the Royal Winnipeg Rifles, the Cameron Highlanders, the 1st Hussars, the Queen's Own Rifles, and from units operating in support of those regiments. It was to become, for the Canadians, the most hated enemy unit in Normandy.

Evidence at Kurt Meyer's trial after the war was not entirely conclusive in establishing that the *Standartenführer* (and later *Brigadeführer* or Major-General) had ordered or even knew about all of these murders; nonetheless, he was held responsible for most of them and sentenced to death, a sentence later commuted to life imprisonment. Probably the prisoners were an impediment to the advancing Germans and were killed because they were in the way; perhaps the NCOs, tough men all, ordered the killings to impress their ruthlessness on their teen-age troops; possibly the SS men, told that the Allies took no prisoners and resentful over the bombings of their homeland, acted in the heat of the moment. That does not lessen the crime. Nor does it help to say that Canadians and other Allied

isoners too. There was a difference between killing in
blooded murder of prisoners hours after the fighting

k had almost wiped out the North Nova Scotia
Fusiliers. After the survivors straggled back to
Buissons, a trench system hastily constructed
North Nova casualties were found to be 84
ed. The Sherbrookes lost 26 killed and 34
tanks destroyed or damaged. The Germans had also paid,
the Sherbrookes claiming up to 35 enemy tanks destroyed. The panzer-grenadier
regiment was thus largely eliminated as an effective force.

The first action of the 9th Brigade had pitted it against a ruthless if equally
inexperienced force and there could be no doubt that the Germans had emerged
the winners. The advance elements of the Canadians had outdistanced their
artillery support, and the brigade's inability to speed help to the North Novas was
critical. The result was that Carpiquet airfield, virtually in view of the leading
units, would not be reached for another month. As for the panzer division, it too
had been handled clumsily, its battalions thrown into the attack piecemeal as they
arrived on the scene. But Kurt Meyer had out-fought the Canadians, and the
fierceness of his attack had left them uncommonly wary of tangling with SS
units.

The SS, however, were hard to avoid. The next day, part of an SS panzer-
grenadier regiment launched itself against the Royal Winnipeg Rifles and the
Regina Rifles. The Winnipegs came under heavy attack at Putot, found themselves almost surrounded and running out of ammunition, and were forced into a
difficult retreat under fire, particularly as the 1st Hussars, stretched thin by the
two previous days' fighting, were unable to lend much assistance. The Reginas
found the enemy turning up in strength behind them at Cairon, and a potential
disaster was averted only by the timely arrival of tanks of the Sherbrooke
Fusiliers.

Brigadier Harry Foster, commanding the 7th Canadian Infantry Brigade,
decided to recapture Putot, and he assigned the task to the Canadian Scottish,
assisted by the guns and mortars of the Cameron Highlanders, the tanks of the 1st
Hussars, and the fire support of two regiments of field artillery. The Scottish
jumped off at 8:30 p.m., just as dusk was settling in, and retook the village, linking
up with remnants of the Winnipegs who, unable to get away earlier that day, had
continued to resist. The Scottish had 45 killed and 80 wounded in taking Putot.
The Winnipegs had lost even more—105 killed and 152 wounded, including most
of the 45 men murdered by the SS on June 8 at the Abbey of Ardenne.

The Regina Rifles also saw heavy fighting that day. In the early evening, German infantry attacked Norrey-en-Bessin, a mile east of Putot, and then turned on the Reginas' main position at Bretteville. Two companies of the Saskatchewan regiment were overrun, and the SS, supported by tanks, broke through the Reginas' lines, penetrating into the regimental headquarters area with their Panther tanks. The resulting brawl was brutal as the Canadians used their short-range PIATs, primitive bazookas, in desperate efforts to cripple the panzers. One German rode through Bretteville on a captured motorcycle and was shot down by Lieutenant-Colonel Foster Matheson, the Reginas' commanding officer; another SS officer drove his Volkswagen up to the battalion headquarters, got out and looked around for a moment, until a Rifleman finished him off with a PIAT bomb. "It was a wild night's work," the official history says, and the battle lasted until morning. However, the Canadian lines, though battered, were still largely intact at dawn.

On the morning of June 9, in fact, tanks of the Fort Garry Horse, attached to the 1st Hussars and supporting the Reginas, caught a column of panzers in line in the open and destroyed them. "We got down the Bretteville-Caen road, with no trouble and put the infantry into the town," the squadron commander of the Fort Garrys wrote shortly before he himself was killed in action, "... when I noticed a hell of a big tank with a long gun pass our front about 900 yards away and going at a good speed. We called up and told the right troops about it, when lo and behold six 'Panthers' came up the crest in orderly fashion. We let them have it and knocked out the six, without them firing a shot at us or traversing their guns in our direction.... We later found out a company of Regina Rifles [at Norrey] had been isolated out there and overrun; these men were saved by our action." The officer added, "We finished off half our D-Day bottle (which I had carefully guarded for weeks for such an occasion) and retired to high ground."

It was a rare day when a Sherman tank could knock out a Panther, and the Fort Garrys' success occurred because the German tanks had been hit on their lightly armoured sides. Some Shermans, the "Fireflies", were armed with 17-pounder guns and could penetrate Panther armour at 600 yards; the ordinary 75mm Sherman shell literally bounced off the Panther. The German tank on the other hand could destroy a Sherman at substantial range, and Canadians grimly referred to their tanks as "Ronsons"—only a spark was necessary to set them alight. The wonder, of course, was that anyone could fight in a tank at all. The Sherman, for example, was 20 feet long, 9 feet wide, and 11 feet high, and it was home to five men, their ammunition, petrol, food and personal gear. The soldiers had difficult and stressful tasks in the metal interior, tasks that had to be accomplished under fire amid a myriad of levers, handles and stanchions.

After two or three days of action, the Canadians of the 3rd Division had discovered how different combat was from their training. They had faced the terrible searching test of battle. They had known the symptoms of fear—pounding heart, a sinking feeling in the stomach, shaking, vomiting, loose bowels. There would be little respite from this fear. Day after day, soldiers would endure shelling, snipers, the hidden menace of anti-personnel mines. They would learn to live without sleep. Once or twice a day, sometimes under fire, men had to dig slit trenches in the hard Normandy clay. One officer summed up his men's experiences:

> Do *you* know what it's like? Of course you don't. You have never slept in a hole in the ground which you have dug while someone tried to kill you…a hole dug as deep as you can as quick as you can.… It is an open grave, and yet graves don't fill with water. They don't harbour wasps or mosquitoes, and you don't feel the cold, clammy wet that goes into your marrow.
>
> At night the infantryman gets some boards, or tin, or an old door and puts it over one end of his slit trench; then he shovels on top of it as much dirt as he can scrape up near by. He sleeps with his head under this, not to keep out the rain, but to protect his head and chest from airbursts. Did I say sleep? Let us say, collapses. You see, the infantryman must be awake for one-half the night. The reason is that one-half of the troops are on watch and the other half are resting, washing, shaving, writing letters, eating, or cleaning weapons; that is if he is not being shot at, shelled, mortared, or counter-attacked or if he is not too much exhausted to do it.

No wonder "battle exhaustion" crippled so many—there were 200 cases in the 3rd Division by June 20.

And the food was always indifferent. Some units like the Queen's Own Rifles had their cooks prepare a hot meal every day and brought it forward to the companies in the line unless the situation made that completely impossible; other units did not make the effort. That meant that the men had to make do with cooking their own, a chancy process at best and one that was almost impossible in action. The armoured units usually prepared their own food with each tank crew responsible for itself. One corporal cook with the Fort Garry Horse circulated a sample series of menus that could be put together from "B" Field Rations, a list that included "Porridge, milk, sugar, Fried bacon, Fried potatoes, Jam, Marg, Bread or biscuits, Tea" for breakfast: "Meat and veg. Pie, deep fried potatoes, Bread pudding, Tea" for dinner; and "Soup, Creamed salmon, Fried potatoes, Veg, Cheese, Bread, Marg, Tea" for supper. That sounded quite lavish, but the cook was probably painting an ideal situation, particularly when he suggested that "instead of just having cheese and biscuits, the cheese can be melted and spread on the biscuits before hand." In action, the infantry and armoured troops more likely opened a can of food, wolfed it down and took a swig of water from a canteen.

When units got out of the front line, the iron hand of military discipline was quick to fall upon them. An account by one squadron commander of the Fort Garrys notes that "a routine part training and part resting and cleaning up, peculiar to the semi-rest area position the Regiment was holding, was adopted. At first, difficulty was experienced in getting the troops to settle down in this more or less static role, and pay close attention to the rules of hygiene and cleanliness, which had been a constant part of their training in England." After fighting for five days or so, in other words, a unit had difficulty in adjusting to the rules and regulations, no matter how sensible they were. Combat was dangerous and potentially fatal; but in a curious way it was more free than being behind the lines.

ROTS AND LE MESNIL

The overall result of the savage fighting on June 8 and June 9 had been a standoff. The Canadian advance had been halted, but Meyer's SS regiment had taken a pasting too, losing dozens of tanks and suffering heavy casualties, and the *Standartenführer* had had to pull his surviving units back to the vicinity of Rots. The 12th SS had been intended to be the spearhead of the German counter-attack, but the spearhead had been blunted.

The reason was simple enough. The great Allied deception had worked. So had the ceaseless, massive air offensive. Hitler and even von Rundstedt and Rommel continued to believe what the Allied planners wanted them to believe—that the major invasion was still destined for the beaches of the Pas de Calais. Divisions cautiously spared for the Normandy front arrived shattered and exhausted after air attacks. Then, because Hitler insisted that every inch of ground be held, the fresh forces were thrown into battle haphazard. By his constant pressure, General Montgomery made sure that the massive armoured counterthrust in von Rundstedt's plan never materialized.

Still, there remained a gap between the 7th and 9th Canadian Infantry Brigades, and the SS panzers at Rots posed a serious threat because of their location and power. An attack on Rots was duly launched on June 11 by a British unit, No. 46 Royal Marine Commando, supported by a company of Chaudières and a squadron of the Fort Garrys. A simple plan had been produced but the result was yet another melee, the SS resisting bitterly. A Fort Garry sergeant wrote of the confused battle in the town:

Major Blanchard was doing a lot of shooting.... He put two of the wounded on his tank and ordered me to follow. As he drove out of the square I told my driver to follow him, but in the confusion my turret had been swung around facing the back of the tank, and the driver was facing the opposite direction, and by the time we turned around the Major was gone.

I tried to follow him, but took the wrong road and headed for enemy territory. The driver had her wide open and when we rounded the corner at the bottom of the street we ran smack into a Panther. The driver...just about stood the tank on her nose, and the gunner...rapped two shots into the Panther at 00 yards setting it on fire. I told my driver to advance around the burning tank but the gunner with the excitement forgot the long-barrelled 17-pounder, and it caught on the burning tank breaking the hand and power traverse. Seeing that we could not bring our gun on any target I told the driver that it was up to him, that speed was what we required....

The sergeant and his crew almost got away but were caught by a Panther. "Just as we stopped and I was halfway out of the turret 'bang' we'd had it. He hit us right in the front." The sergeant made his way back to Canadian lines but most of his crew was killed or captured. Another survivor, Captain Eddie Goodman, had been given up for lost when, burned but unfazed, he showed up to demand a new tank. The town of Rots was now in Allied hands, 122 Germans being buried there.

The same day, June 11, a few miles away, the Canadians attacked the village of Le Mesnil-Patry, using a combined force of tanks from the 1st Hussars and infantry from the Queen's Own Rifles. A Queen's Own lieutenant, Ben Dunkelman, was charged with providing mortar-fire support for the attack. He was waiting at the start line to work out details when tanks, with the infantry clinging on, roared past. The infantry could not get off to adopt their assault formation, and, Dunkelman recalled, "It began to look as if the [tank commander] had never heard of the word 'co-ordinate'! We were ready to lay down fire from our two mortar platoons, as well as from two regiments of artillery—and here he was charging at the enemy unsupported. Effective supporting fire was out of the question now, because we didn't know the precise advance route and were afraid of hitting our own men. They were on their own."

The result was a disaster. Within moments, the tanks came under German fire. Infantry had to clamber off under the worst conditions, far short of the objective. Raw courage got some of the tanks and the infantry into Le Mesnil, but the German armour and infantry brought their anti-tank weapons into play. The key weapon was the 88mm gun, the most feared weapon of the war to Allied troops.

("It was a staggering thing, in size, just a beautiful piece of death and destruction for us in the tanks," one armoured regiment survivor remembered, sounding almost wistful about the weapon that destroyed so many Canadian tanks.) An order for the 1st Hussars to pull back apparently never arrived. The lead squadron was annihilated, with 19 of its tanks destroyed and only 2 reaching safety. The Queen's Own had done its best. A lieutenant, although twice wounded in the initial phase, organized a party of 9 riflemen and 2 tanks and shot up the town with great effect. "I have never witnessed a battle of this intensity, before or since," Dunkelman wrote. The infantry lost 55 dead and 44 wounded, the 1st Hussars, in their worst experience of the war, lost 59 killed and 21 wounded. "It was," wrote a British newspaper of Le Mesnil-Patry, "a modern version of the charge of the Light Brigade." It was just about as futile.

The battle at Le Mesnil-Patry brought to an end the battle of the bridgehead, and the 3rd Canadian Division was not engaged in further major actions until the beginning of July. That was a function of General Montgomery's strategy for the battle, but it was probably also a result of the heavy casualties the Canadians had suffered. During the first six days of the invasion, 1017 of them had died. Whole units had been battered severely, in particular the Queen's Own, the North Novas, the Winnipegs and Reginas and the 1st Hussars. That was the price of making the Canadian share of the bridgehead secure.

REST AND RESPITE

The American and British bridgeheads were solid, too. The Americans had finally managed to link up the Utah and Omaha beachheads and to drive inland. Here the dream of a speedy advance turned into a nightmare in the *bocage* of rural Normandy, where every hedgerow provided perfect cover for the defenders. The masses of American armour were not very useful in such circumstances. As a result the American attempts to take Cherbourg and its vitally needed port were delayed. By June 17-18, however, American forces had finally cut the Cotentin peninsula, isolating Cherbourg. On June 26, after a bitter struggle, the city fell. Unfortunately, the defenders had systematically destroyed the port facilities, making the harbour almost useless.

A safe harbour was a matter of crucial importance. Next to D-Day itself, the greatest risk to the Normandy invasion was the possibility that storms could cut off supplies. That was why the huge Mulberry harbours had been built and towed laboriously to their anchorages off the beaches. Now disaster struck. An Atlantic storm blew up the channel on June 19, and for four days high waves battered the Mulberries. By June 23, the American Mulberry was wrecked, the British Mulberry at Arromanches was damaged and hundreds of landing craft were beached or sunk.

To June 18, the Allies had successfully landed 621,986 men and 95,750 vehicles, along with 217,624 tons of stores. No more could come ashore until the great storm had abated. Even so, by June 30—24 days after D-Day—Allied troops in France had reached the impressive total of 861,838 men supported by 157,633 vehicles and 501,834 tons of supplies and ammunition.

By late June, the course of the battle had created acrimony among the Allies as staff officers at the Supreme Headquarters of the Allied Expeditionary Force (SHAEF) began to grumble at the slow progress made by the British and Canadians before Caen. The attacks in that sector did not seem to be pressed forward with sufficient determination. Even the Germans thought so, though they moved most of their armoured units to face Montgomery's British and Canadian divisions. In England it seemed that only the Americans were making gains.

The Germans, however, were far from hopeful about their own position. On the contrary. When Rommel and von Rundstedt met Hitler, in the Führer's fleeting visit to France on June 17, they stated that the Allies were ashore and could not be driven out of France. On June 29, the two field-marshals again saw the Führer. Again Hitler rejected their arguments that the line in Normandy could not be held much longer. At this point, so Rundstedt told Canadian interrogators after the surrender, he had shouted at another officer who had asked, "What shall we do?" the obvious but unwelcome reply, "Make peace, you idiots! What else can you do?" Peace was not on Hitler's agenda.

Meanwhile, General Crerar had crossed the channel and set up a small headquarters in Amblie. Montgomery had been forced to postpone the completion of the First Canadian Army in Normandy because of the delay in capturing Caen. There was simply no room in the crowded beachhead for additional units. The 2nd Canadian Infantry Division would arrive in early July but, until it did, II Canadian Corps could not be operational either. Crerar's headquarters—and Lieutenant-General Guy Simonds' Corps headquarters—had to wait their turns.

The respite from action let the units of the 3rd Canadian Infantry Division restore themselves. The Queen's Own Rifles received 62 reinforcements on June 19, only to discover, as the history of the regiment observes drily, that "the greater number of these men were not trained infantry men. Indeed, only a few knew how to operate a Bren gun. So quick courses in basic training had to start immediately." The battalions survived, but the losses in the D-Day battles could never quite be filled by surplus cooks, mechanics and gunners from the depots in England. Already, within weeks of the landing, the manpower crisis of 1944 was beginning to be felt by the Canadian army in Europe.

As part of the long wait, a Canadian chaplain holds a service on the top deck of a Landing Ship Tank. "Padres" (as the army called them) had a tough role in an organization that was nominally Christian but whose members came from all faiths or none. Chaplains, too, came in all sizes but the most successful were those who shared the lives and fears of the men they served. (PA132899/Public Archives Canada)

A gunner of the Royal Canadian Artillery and a sergeant from the Cameron Highlanders of Ottawa eat a last meal before their landing ship heads for the beaches. Veterans will remember the experience of seeing soup, meat, vegetables and maybe a piece of pie dumped in the same oblong aluminum messtin. "It'll all look like that in your stomach" was the standard answer to complainers. (PA132654/Public Archives Canada)

This is what Juno Beach looked like to a photographer in the second wave of assault craft. The sea was rough, the sky cloudy and thick smoke rose along the length of the beach. As boats got closer, the sounds of battle were almost deafening. It was like nothing any of their training had led them to expect. (Author's collection)

OVERLEAF: Sailors on the *Prince Henry* help a British survivor from a sunken landing craft climb aboard. General Eisenhower's decision to go ahead with the invasion was probably right but it disregarded a choppy sea and the risk of storms. Even for experts, handling a landing craft in a rough sea was no picnic, and many of the crews were still learning. Beach obstacles and enemy fire also caused heavy losses in the assault waves. (PA132788/Public Archives Canada)

A Landing Craft (Assault) from the Canadian ship *Prince Henry* batters down the waves as it heads for the beaches while its infantry passengers anxiously await their ordeal. In the background, Canadian frigates from the bombardment force attend fire orders. (PA132790/Public Archives Canada)

At last they are going in. LCAs from a landing ship offshore head for Juno beach carrying men of one of the Canadian assault battalions, the Royal Winnipeg Rifles. These are men going into battle and they have some powerful worrying to do. (PA132651/Public Archives Canada)

German beach defences were built around carefully fortified posts like this machine-gun nest. While the concrete pillbox shows the marks of shelling, the machine-gun, like many other German weapons on Juno beach, survived intact. Assault troops had to tackle such weapons themselves. Note the assault ladder, welded from pipe, and the thick barbed wire. A reserve platoon from Le Régiment de la Chaudière waits its turn to advance over the wall and into St. Aubin-sur-Mer. (PA116532/Public Archives Canada)

Tanks of the 1st Hussars, a regiment from London, Ontario, pour ashore on the afternoon of D-Day. Already, Royal Canadian Engineers are busy trying to keep the beach passable with the aid of an armoured bulldozer. Clearing the beach of men and vehicles was a huge task, particularly since planners had exaggerated the likely speed of the advance inland and underestimated the physical problems of getting off beaches onto solid land. Yet only by enlarging the beachhead could they save it from the inevitable German counter-attacks. (PA128791/Public Archives Canada)

OVERLEAF: Afternoon on Juno Beach: after the first wave has pushed inland, the reserve brigades pour from Landing Craft (Infantry) onto the beaches of Bernières-sur-Mer. By dusk, these soldiers of the North Nova Scotia Highlanders and the Highland Light Infantry will be in the line and under fire. (PA122765/Public Archives Canada)

A Canadian three-ton truck heads for shore from a landing craft. Canvas screens under the radiator are part of the effort to waterproof the engine so that the truck could wade through water over its axles. A white five-pointed star was a common recognition sign for all Allied vehicles. The conspicuous mark on the roof was evidence that drivers now had more to fear from friendly planes than from the Luftwaffe. White splotches cover whatever the censor judged "hush hush". (PA132804/Public Archives Canada)

On the day after D-Day—or D+1, June 7—a tracked light anti-aircraft gun
awaits for the Luftwaffe next to a disabled DD tank. The canvas curtain was
intended to help the tank float, while a small propeller geared to the tank
engine gave the amphibious tank both its name (Duplex Drive) and its motive
power through the water. A fine idea in calm seas, DD tanks were not meant
for the rough water they faced on June 6 and most of the Canadian tanks that
reached the beaches landed "dry-shod". (PA132897/Public Archives Canada)

Not everything (or everyone) got ashore. A German shell caught this Canadian Bren gun carrier as it headed for land. There were no survivors. Behind it are vehicles that "drowned" on the way to the beach, and, in the distance, the wreckage of landing craft holed on German beach obstacles and sunk. (PA132895/Public Archives Canada)

Canadian infantry reinforcements wade ashore past a Landing Craft (Tank)
beached at low tide. These men lack the distinctively shaped steel helmet issued
to Canadian soldiers in the assault waves. Devised by Canadian engineers as a
better combination of comfort and protection than the familiar "wash basin", it
was eventually adopted by the British army and abandoned by the Canadians.
(PA132655/Public Archives Canada)

OVERLEAF: The German high command considered the divisions posted to
beach defences expendable. Many of the soldiers were East Europeans, given
the choice of serving in Hitler's Wehrmacht or wasting away in his prison
camps. But officers and sergeants and some of the men were Germans and they
fought hard. This group of prisoners, headed by two German officers, is a fair
sample of the enemy Canadians met at Bernières-sur-Mer. (PA114493/Public
Archives Canada)

No one asked the people of Normandy whether they wanted their part of France liberated first. Chances are they would have allowed the honour to go elsewhere. While a British assault vehicle prepares to demolish any further signs of resistance, two citizens of Bernières-sur-Mer wheel away all they can rescue from their wrecked homes. (PA132725/Public Archives Canada)

Once the war had passed by, life in the Norman villages slowly returned to normal. For these two children, normality meant playing soldiers with a British helmet and a discarded Canadian officer's cap. Canadian soldiers remembered youngsters they had left behind and wondered whether they would ever see them again. (PA132724/Public Archives Canada)

Armoured vehicles stop to give their crews a breather. Unlike infantry,
who had to carry everything they needed, soldiers with vehicles had a
mechanical monster to carry their food, bedding and other necessities.
A little brutal experience taught them that bedrolls could catch fire from
an enemy incendiary bullet, the flames would sweep into an engine

air intake and the result would be a "brew-up". Infantry who stood by helplessly as a crew was roasted in a burning tank or armoured car soon lost any envy for those who could "bus to battle". As for the crews, they soon learned that spare track welded to the hull beefed up the inadequate armour of their fighting vehicles.

After the savage battle for a foothold in Normandy, Canadian infantry would face the brunt of a German counter-attack: that was the grim message Major-General R.F.L. Keller, commanding the 3rd Canadian Division, had to impress

on his men on the afternoon of D-Day. One reason the 3rd Division had been chosen for the critical assault was that Keller was believed to be one of the ablest Canadian senior officers. (PA115544/Public Archives Canada)

As soon as the first landing strips could be established, air force Dakotas flew seriously sick and wounded casualties back to England. That emptied the beds of field hospitals and got soldiers to first-class medical facilities within a couple of hours. All Allied aircraft involved in the D-Day landings bore three wide white stripes as identification. (PA132880/Public Archives Canada)

An Orders Group near Vieux Cairon on June 20, as Lieutenant-Colonel F.M. Griffiths of the Highland Light Infantry of Canada tells his officers what comes next. Though Griffiths' battalion had not yet suffered heavy losses, lieutenants were already commanding companies and sergeants were in charge of platoons. The cost of battle was beginning to show. (PA116520/Public Archives Canada)

OVERLEAF: Away from the beaches, Normandy in June was a warm, leafy green paradise for troops who were utterly sick of the grey, heaving sea. Infantry rest by the side of the road while a column of Shermans, with a French tricolour flying from the aerial of the leading tank, rumbles down a country road. Time would teach Canadians that leafy trees hid snipers and roadside ditches had sometimes been sown with German anti-personnel mines. (PA132801/Public Archives Canada)

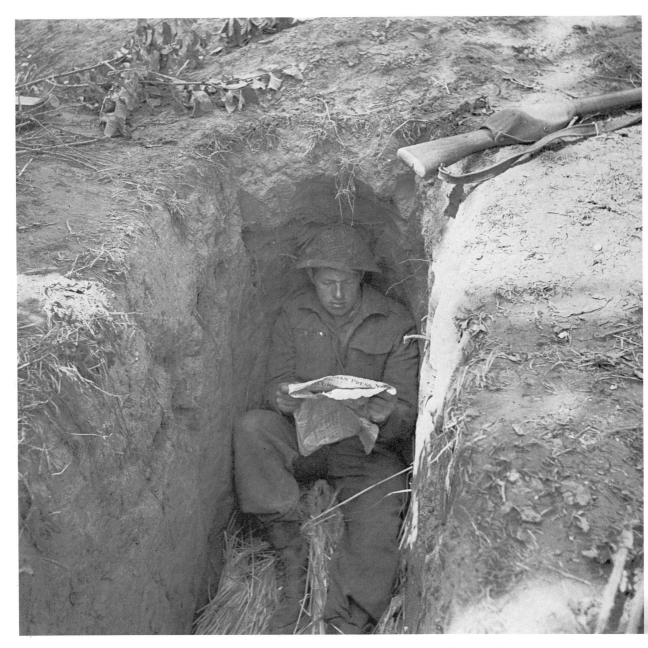

If American soldiers dug foxholes, Canadians had their slit-trenches. This soldier is far enough behind the line to make only a few feeble efforts at camouflage, and the breechcover on his rifle will keep it clean for inspection, if not readily available. Since, as soldiers said, there was no prize for being miserable, a little straw "liberated" from a nearby barn makes for more comfortable waiting. The *Canadian Press News* was printed in England and flown to France. (PA129039/Public Archives Canada)

Private B. McGeough of the Canadian Scottish did not find this leg of pork in the M&V of the official compo ration. Like soldiers of all eras, he helped himself and settled down to prepare dinner. A ration box, with its familiar shamrock label, served as a kitchen counter. Senior officers might deplore the fact, but Canadian soldiers found that a little resourcefulness and hard work eased the hardships of active service. (M&V = meat and vegetables, though veterans will remember damned little of either.) (PA132884/Public Archives Canada)

"Monty and Johnny" was a familiar feature in *The Maple Leaf*. Created by Les Callan, a cartoonist with pre-war experience in Winnipeg, Toronto and Vancouver, the drawings feature the familiar soldier themes of homesickness, pompous superiors and ingenuity in the face of adversity. (*The Maple Leaf Scrapbook*, p.5)

FOR CANADIAN TROOPS

THE MAPLE LEAF

With Canadian Press News Service

FRANCE EDITION

Vol. 1, No. 1.   FRANCE, July 27, 1944

OUR TROOPS IN HARD FIGHTING

Reds Advance take Narva fight for Lvov

RUSSIAN

The Russians have taken Narva, seven miles inside Estonia and pushed 10 miles beyond, it was announced today.

Further south, they have driven deep into the heart of Lithian 100 miles from the Baltic coast.

Other Soviet troops reached the Vistula on a wide front to a place within 50 miles of Warsaw.

The announcement said that the Russians have cut the enemy's last escape railway out of Brest-Litovsk. In the South they broke into the suburbs of Lvov where the Germans are now completely encircled.

Beyond St. Lo

American tanks have smashed a 5 mile wedge into the German defences west of St. Lo. They have captured the village of St. Gilles and the town of Marigny on the road leading west from St. Lo to the big road centre of Coutances.

HERE WE GO AGAIN!

HI YAH CANADA! COMMENT ALLEZ-VOUS?

MAPLE LEAF FRANCE EDITION

NORMANDY

Butter thick for French people but bread still slices thin

BY M. DESJARDINS
The Canadian Press

How is the civilian population of liberated Normandy faring after more than six weeks of a new German-free life?

I have talked to dozens of people and from these conversations can be obtained a fair picture of the situation.

Meat is plentiful. Even under the Nazi Regime the Normans were eating well and clandestine slaughtering of cattle took place. Bread offers a more serious problem.

Normandy has always relied on other provinces of France for its wheat since the liberated area does not produce enough wheat for its own needs.

Grain reserves are exhausted and now bakers have become dealers in hardtack.

FOOD SCARCE

The homeless from the south are flocking to villages in the narrow beach areas where houses still have roofs.

Villages with normal populations of 200 now have in some cases more than 700 to feed. Food reserves do not last long under these conditions.

There is more butter now than before the invasion and grocers retail it at reasonable prices.

Milk is harder to find. The farmer has discovered that the troops like milk and sells it to them at ten cents or more a glass.

It is a mild form of black market.

Farmers keep most of their eggs and sell the rest to soldiers at ten cents apiece – more black market.

Many a wheat field has been razed by our war machines, but rich crops are expected in fields which stand outside the immediate zone of battle.

The one thing the Norman fears above bombs and shells is having to drink water. He has been over generous with his cider and his reserves are getting tragically low. It will be three or four months before he can again squeeze his apples.

When the Germans were here the tobacco rations were infinitesimal. Four packages of cigarettes a month. The Normans used to grow some tobacco plants in their gardens but this is an art and the leaves they reaped produced foul cigarettes. However, with our lavish hand-outs they are smoking quite regularly.

Three years for forger

OTTAWA, July 25 — Frederick George Comrie, fifty year old former assistant treasurer of War Services Department was sentenced by Judge MacDougall to three years imprisonment on 25 charges involving theft, forgery, and uttering of cheques. Sergeant Detective William H. Styran told the court the total amount of cheques involved in all charges was in the vicinity of three thousand dollars.

There were eleven charges of forgery, one of uttering and thirteen of theft.

Comrie attributed his acts to financial difficulties brought about he said, by being transferred from Calgary where he maintained a home to Ottawa.

"In Ottawa we got into debt," he said. "I had no intention of hiding anything."

Births !!!

Bern: To Rose and Steve Munro, a daughter. Ross Munro is a well known Canadian war correspondent. Steve is the well known Canadian nursing sister he married. She is now in Canada. Congratulations!

Canadian Research

OTTAWA — Agriculture Minister Gardiner, in a recent speech in the Commons, said that plans are well advanced for the establishment of a wool research laboratory to investigate values of wool fibres in relation to breeding of sheep.

Lethbridge Alberta has been decided as the best place to establish the laboratory as most of the high quality wool breeds of sheep now are in southern Alberta and Saskatchewan.

He said that the Government will continue this year to experiment with the recovery of marsh lands in Nova Scotia and New Brunswick. A thousand dollars was spent last year on recovery experiments.

The minister said that the codling moths were a serious threat to apple orchards in the Okanagan Valley of British Columbia and were causing considerable damage to orchards in Nova Scotia, Ontario and Quebec. New methods are being used in an attempt to control the pest.

Enemy Counters To Regain Ground

By CHARLES LYNCH
Reuter Special Correspondent

With the Canadians in Normandy, July 27 — On Tuesday the Canadians broke into the strongest German defences on the rim of the beachhead, and yesterday battled to hold what they had gained. Some ground had been given up last night.

That is the way a spokesman summed up the picture on the Canadian front.

To the soldiers it has been two days of blood and death and whistling shells and an almost continuous roar of explosions as these boys from the Dominion fought their way uphill to flush the Jerries out of their trenches and pillboxes and dug in tanks.

The main front was about three miles wide three miles of wheatfields and hedges and gullies and shattered villages where the Germans made their first determined stand since Canadian and British troops hurled them out of their strongholds north of Caen.

It was high ground that the Canadians assaulted, with the Germans looking down and the Canadians looking up.

German gun positions looked down on the Canadians from the front and from the right, across the river Orne.

Canadian guns have fired smoke shells into these German positions across the Orne in an effort to blind the enemy gunners — but said the mortar fire pours across.

The heaviest fighting took place yesterday and last night. Today, both sides are collecting themselves and most of the activity is mortaring and shelling.

The Canadian infantry launched the attack in the pitch blackness of 0300 hours Tuesday.

The Germans fought bitterly from the outset, and few prisoners were taken.

It was a three-pronged attack behind a creeping artillery barrage.

Moving along the line of the road running from Caen to the famous shrine of Falaise, the Canadians battled their way into the shattered villages of Tilly la Campagne, Verrieres and May Sur Orne.

While the troops were going in, Allied medium bombers gave a wood to the east of the advance a shellacking, hitting at a concentration of enemy guns. Rocket-firing Typhoons roamed the area behind the German lines, shooting up transport wherever they could find it.

The Germans, who had been strengthening their positions on the high ground for the last week, reacted quickly to the attack and shortly after dawn were counter-attacking May Verrieres and Tilley.

This first counter-attacks were beaten off — but the Germans brought in their armour and drove in again and again.

Vicious fighting went on all day and last night. Dawn Wednesday saw the Germans holding May Sur Orne and most of Tilly, with the Canadians sitting firmly in Verrieres.

Canadian and British tanks, guns and plit mortars combined to take a toll of German tanks which were milling around the battlefield all day.

While this fighting on the Canadian sector was at its height, the Americans in the St. Lo sector far to the west staged a large-scale assault, and broke into the German lines in several places. — Heavy and medium bombers sent thousands of tons of high explosives into the German positions to soften them up for the attack.

Elsewhere, the american front was quiet, with the Germans awaiting General Montmo.

MAPLE LEAF DELIVERY

The Maple Leaf is distributed free to all Canadian forces in the theatre on the basis of one copy per seven men. It will require a few issues to get the delivery system going a hundred per cent. If your platoon, section or H.Q. does not get its proper allotment go to your postal corporal about it and see whether or not your unit is getting its regular bundle. If not get him to scream about it and let us know — we will see that you get on our list pronto.

Separate bundles are made up for each unit and will be delivered on the same day as publication in the forward post offices. After picking up to your unit to ensure dividing up between platoons and detachments.

The Maple Leaf was the Canadian Army's official newspaper for troops in the field. It first appeared in Italy in 1943. A Normandy edition appeared within weeks of the capture of Caen, using the presses of a local newspaper. While the brass kept a closer eye on content than anyone admitted, the paper was run by professional newspaper people who happened to find themselves in uniform.

Kurt Meyer commanded the SS troops who hit the Canadians head-on on June 7. Like other senior officers of the 12th *Hitlerjugend* Division, Meyer had been handpicked as an ideal Nazi soldier. Compare the neat young officer of 1941, freshly decorated by Hitler with the Knight's Cross, and the weary battle-hardened veteran of the Russian front three years later. More than anyone, Meyer would be the Canadian nemesis during the long, deadly Normandy campaign. (Ullstein Bilderdienst 44999, 44999d)

This young German prisoner, sullen pride still evident, was typical of the
youthful *Hitlerjugend* troops from the 12th SS who were the first and toughest
enemies Canadians faced in the fighting after D-Day. The German camouflage
suit was envied by Canadian snipers like the soldier holding this prisoner.
(Author's collection)

III
Struggle
for Caen

The great D-Day gamble had paid off. Huge resources, planning, courage and a lot of luck had delivered a Normandy beachhead at far lower cost than almost anyone had estimated.

Yet, once ashore, the Canadians alone had come even close to their D-Day objectives, only to be driven back by a wall of German resistance. Throughout June, the lines hardly moved though Allied planes routed the Luftwaffe and decimated German armoured divisions approaching the battle. Among SHAEF planners, the fear grew that, as in the landings at Anzio and Salerno in the Italian campaign, fast German reactions had contained the invaders. Dreams of a Second Front shrivelled. Blame was easily placed. American and RAF critics complained that Montgomery was too cautious and plodding to be a great commander. An aggressive general would have had offensives exploding all along the beachhead perimeter.

Montgomery was cautious but he was also shrewd. Photographs of Rommel and von Rundstedt stared from the walls of his caravan. Montgomery tried to understand how their minds worked. The Germans would expect him to attack down the road from Caen through Falaise to Paris. Von Rundstedt would dismiss the raw, boastful Americans as no real threat.

Von Rundstedt's illusion was to be fostered as carefully as the elaborate ruse that persuaded the German High Command to wait for another, bigger invasion in the Pas de Calais. Months before D-Day, Montgomery had made it clear that General Omar Bradley's First United States Army would carry out the break-through. For this to happen General Miles Dempsey's Second British Army must divert and hold the crack German panzer divisions in its sector.

As supreme commander, Eisenhower had approved Montgomery's strategy though he never entirely agreed with it. He would have been happier if every division had pushed forward. Unlike Montgomery, Eisenhower had been spared the First World War, with its pointless, murderous offensives. Bled white in that war, Britain now lacked the young men to replace its losses. The Canadians, dependent on volunteers to fill their ranks, were almost as worried. Montgomery's mandate was to use strategy to cut the tragic costs.

Moreover, Montgomery's strategy worked. The German commanders agreed that Caen was crucial. Each time they began to muster panzer divisions for a mortal blow at the beachhead, a British or Canadian thrust near Caen forced them to change priorities. Ordinary soldiers paid the bloody price of fighting some of the finest troops and weapons in Hitler's army. A public thirsting for quick, easy victories gave no glory to such sacrifice.

Despite private misgivings, Eisenhower backed his prickly subordinate. German generals had no such support: from his bunker in East Prussia, Hitler dictated strategy and tactics. Common sense told Rommel and von Rundstedt to retreat beyond the range of the Allied naval guns, using the dense Norman countryside to exact a terrific toll from the advancing Allies, but Hitler refused. His own will was strong enough to uphold the entire German people. Not an inch of Normandy would be given up and each attack must be met by counter-attack. The allies would be destroyed. For their defeatism, generals would be removed—or worse.

Meanwhile, the Führer proclaimed, he would win the battle of supply. The Luftwaffe would defend "safe corridors" through which men, equipment and munitions would pour into the battle. His promise failed utterly. Half the 600 fighters, switched from the defence of Germany, were gone in two weeks. Though tank production boomed in Germany, almost none of it reached Normandy; Allied bombers and the French Resistance saw to that. Barely 10,000 men arrived to replace the 100,000 German casualties in the first six weeks of the campaign.

In the end, all that sustained Hitler's strategy was the skill and sacrifice of his troops and their brilliant use of the Norman countryside. Few soldiers anywhere, fighting week after week, blasted from the air, suffering endless heavy losses, could have tolerated what German Wehrmacht and SS formations endured. The terrain worked to their advantage. Almost a thousand years before, Celtic farmers had planted the hedgerows and laid out the narrow roads of the *bocage* country. Centuries-old root systems defied even tanks and bulldozers. Ample cover hid an enemy's machine-guns and anti-tank weapons. South of Caen, where the country opened into rolling wheat fields, ancient stone farms and villages made natural fortresses for tough panzer-grenadiers and their incredible array of weapons. Few Allied planners had foreseen the problems of fighting in such terrain.

LEARNING ABOUT WAR

In Normandy, Canadian soldiers had no voice in strategy. They were its instruments, struggling to find the tactics to fight an enemy that always seemed better trained and far better armed. A few weeks of fierce combat had transformed the 3rd Canadian Division and the 2nd Armoured Brigade from neat, efficient formations that won praise from visiting generals into battle-wise veterans, ragged and dirty survivors. Never, in three years of training, had they learned faster; they now knew how to dig, spread out, spot minefields and pray.

On paper, infantry battalions mustered over eight hundred men; few went into battle with even half that strength. Soldiers in action saw little more than their section of six or seven men or their platoon of twenty. Its commander, a lieutenant or, more often in battle, a sergeant, got his orders from a company commander, a major or captain. Behind the four rifle companies of an infantry battalion, its colonel could count on a reserve of firepower in his support company: mortars, anti-tank guns and a platoon of lightly armed and armoured carriers to haul weapons, distribute ammunition or rescue the wounded.

At Le Mesnil-Patry, the 1st Hussars had discovered how helpless their American-made Shermans were against the heavy German Tiger and Panther tanks. Men trapped with broken arms and legs after a deadly shot from a German 88mm gun died horribly when the flammable "Ronsons" burned. Though nothing could hide the Sherman's high, ungainly silhouette, tank crews hurriedly welded lengths of track to hulls to thicken inadequate armour and laid sandbags on the tank floor to keep legs from breaking when a mine exploded. Troopers who had used gasoline to dry-clean their battledress realized why some had turned into human torches in a "brew-up".

Allied planners knew the weakness of the Sherman—that was the price of mass-production—but fresh tanks were pouring onto the beaches in numbers that would swamp the superior German models. There were other excellent Allied weapons, though many were far behind the front lines. German prisoners, dismayed by the rate of artillery fire, sometimes pleaded to see the automatic loading devices on the Canadian 25-pounder field guns. What they saw were sweating, cursing Canadian gunners, ramming home shells as fast as a distant battery commander, close to the front line, could wish. Germans also envied the tough, dependable 60-cwt trucks, built in Canada for British armies everywhere, faithfully hauling far more than their official load.

The real Allied tactical advantage was in the air. The British and Canadian squadrons of 83 Group flew Spitfires, Mustangs, Typhoons, whatever was needed to flatten the Luftwaffe and back the infantry. To Allied soldiers, the Typhoon was the wonder-weapon of the campaign; to Germans, it was the one terror weapon. Veteran pilots flew it in the teeth of German flak, killing tanks with armour-piercing rockets as no other weapon could. On the bright, clear summer days of 1944, the "Tiffie" made the difference.

In the cramped beachhead, medical and supply units were set up. Trucks of the Royal Canadian Army Service Corps crawled along the narrow Norman roads delivering food, gasoline and ammunition. Occasional devastating blasts and plumes of smoke showed where luckless drivers had hit mines. Medical units collected sick and wounded from Regimental Aid Posts just behind the lines. Jeep ambulance drivers preferred speed; the wounded suffered the agony of a rough ride. By now, army doctors had easy access to penicillin to control infection and plasma to save dying soldiers. On the other hand, far more of the wounded than in the 1914-18 war had been torn apart by mortar or artillery shells or terribly burned in tank "brew-ups". By the end of June, three thousand Canadian sick and wounded had left for England; many more stayed for treatment as Canadian hospitals spread their tents at Secqueville or around Bayeux—an area British soldiers soon christened "Harley Street".

In theory, the age-old problem of control on the battlefield had been solved by the use of wireless. From companies through battalions, brigades, divisions, corps, armies and across to armoured and artillery regiments, messages crackled invisibly. But the miracle was fallible. Wireless sets were heavy, big and vulnerable. The army—even the headquarters—had no link with friendly air forces and anything from stray shrapnel to atmospherics could dissolve the command network. Always, too, the Germans were listening. It took time for Canadian officers to learn the cost of babbling orders and locations. Meanwhile, German intelligence had not only learned Canadian battle codes and organization, but had worked out how to give occasional persuasive commands.

By July, the other Canadian divisions—the 2nd and the 4th Armoured—would arrive in Normandy, full of fresh confidence to learn about war the hard, cruel way. "Who has not fought the Germans," said an old soldiers' slogan, "has not fought." The Canadians would fight the Germans and, in due course, they would win.

CARPIQUET

First, they had more to learn. So did the British. West of the Orne River Montgomery had planned the first of the "controlled attacks" to hold the

Germans on the British front. Delayed by the Channel storm, Operation Epsom began on June 26 when two raw British divisions, the 15th Scottish and the 11th Armoured, started to drive across the Odon and the Orne to threaten Caen. They made it only part-way. Two fresh panzer divisions, arriving unexpectedly under cover of the bad weather, launched a devastating counter-attack. Warned by "Ultra", their super-secret decoding system, the British were ready. Sudden sunshine sent Typhoons pouring in for the kill. Young Scottish conscripts, caught in the narrow corridor of their advance, held their lines. By June 29, Epsom was over.

Though Hitler claimed a triumph, his generals knew otherwise. A despairing von Rundstedt offered the only advice he believed: withdraw. On July 2, he was replaced by Field-Marshal Günther von Kluge, a Hitler favourite with a reputation for defensive victories in Russia. His loyalty to the Führer rested on his personal oath and a gift from Hitler of 140,000 reichsmarks.

On July 4, it was the Canadians' turn to attack. Partly rested, Major-General Rod Keller's 3rd Division was given a simple enough task: capture Carpiquet airport. It was held by only 150 boys from Kurt Meyer's 12th SS but the Canadians had no illusions. Operation Windsor would demand four battalions— Brigadier Ken Blackader's 8th Brigade of the North Shores, the Chaudières and the Queen's Own, plus the Royal Winnipeg Rifles for a separate attack on the south side of the field. Tanks of the Fort Garry Horse, engineer assault vehicles, a flame-throwing Crocodile tank and all the artillery the division could muster would back the attack.

In the event, it seemed little enough. At dawn, the Canadians rose, crossed the start line and walked into fields of waist-high wheat. Suddenly, their rolling artillery barrage seemed to stop moving forward. Some Canadians never lived to learn that the Germans had dumped their shells on the Canadian barrage line; they probably died thinking they were killed by their own side. The rest kept going, pausing only to mark the bodies of dead and wounded with a symbol that soon sprouted quickly on the field—a bayoneted rifle jabbed into the dirt.

At Carpiquet village, survivors from the North Shores and the Chaudières waged pitiless warfare in the ruins. "*On ne fit aucun prisonnier ce jour-là,*" confessed Captain Michel Gauvin, a future diplomat. For the North Shores, it was the bloodiest day of the campaign: 132 casualties, 46 of them dead. "That first night alone," the padre of the North Shores wrote, "we buried 40 of our boys. You could fancy the wheat field had once been just like any wheat field back home. Now it was torn with shell holes and everywhere you could see the pale upturned faces of the dead." On the opposite side of the airfield, the Winnipeggers fared even worse. For them, there was no cover at all. Pillboxes and concrete bunkers, built long before by the Luftwaffe, allowed the Germans to sweep the approaches. Guns and tanks blasted the attackers and when Captain Alec Christian of the Garrys brought his squadron forward, half his tanks were destroyed. Twice the Winnipeggers surged forward; twice they stopped. At dusk, Lieutenant-Colonel J.M. Meldram was ordered to bring the remnant of his battalion back.

Keller fumed but his men could do no more. At night, the Canadians in Carpiquet were deluged by artillery and mortar fire. A company of Chaudières was overrun and few escaped. Later, some of the Canadians were found, bound, shot and buried. At dawn, the last German counter-attack was driven off. Operation Windsor was incomplete but somehow the men who held Carpiquet felt mildly triumphant. The cost was high: of perhaps 2,000 men engaged, 371 were casualties, and more than 100 were dead.

CAEN

Montgomery and the British corps commander were harshly critical of the Canadians and their commander, General Keller, for the failure at Carpiquet. Generals far in the rear complained that the Canadians were no longer as bold or as well led as they had been on the D-Day beaches. The savage fight at Carpiquet was a warning. A dozen such villages surrounded the ancient Norman city and each could take such a toll. Yet, if Montgomery's strategy was to remain credible, Caen had to be taken. Eisenhower applied tactful pressure. RAF officers, like his SHAEF deputy Sir Arthur Tedder, were blunter: Montgomery's caution was costing them airfields they needed south-east of Caen.

If the air force wanted an attack, perhaps it could help. Air Chief Marshal Sir Arthur Harris of Bomber Command was agreeable, but on his terms. To ensure the troops' safety, the bomb line would be set 6,000 yards in front of British and Canadian positions. Instead of preceding a dawn assault, set for July 8, weather predictions dictated that bombs be dropped the night before.

For assaulting troops, the raid at 10:30 p.m. on July 7 was a spectacular morale-booster. "We watched waves of bombers come in from England," an intelligence officer later wrote, "pouring out of the setting sun like a gigantic swarm of bees about to take over the world; passing overhead with a beat of thunder that shook the ground...." The roar and flames as 467 bombers dumped 2,561 tons of explosive on the stricken city convinced nervous soldiers that their battle was half-won. In fact, few Germans were in Caen, and fewer of them were among the 400 dead or the thousands injured. Germans in the fortified villages outside Caen were also outside Harris's bomb line. In hindsight, the bombing of Caen was a hideous, futile tragedy of war.

Not bombers but artillery assisted the assaulting divisions forward. Every gun in General Dempsey's Second British Army and many of those off shore joined the barrage. For assault troops of the 3rd Canadian Division, some of the objectives were painfully familiar. So was the enemy: Meyer's 12th SS. At Buron, the Highland Light Infantry from southwestern Ontario, unbloodied in the month since D-Day, lost 262 men and their colonel in a day-long battle. By then, the North Novas had come back to Authie where so many had died on D-Day-plus-1. As the 9th Brigade pushed south at Keller's urging, Brigadier Harry Foster's 7th Brigade headed for Cussy and the Abbey of Ardenne, Meyer's headquarters. Long past nightfall, the Regina Rifles and the Sherbrooke Fusiliers struggled against Meyer's men. Lurid flames from burning Canadian and German tanks lit the sky.

By dawn, Meyer and his men were gone. The German front might have held but, far to the right, a raw division formed from surplus Luftwaffe men had collapsed before the regulars of the 3rd British Division. On July 9, men of Brigadier Dan Cunningham's Highland Brigade worked their way cautiously into Caen. Snipers, mines and booby traps slowed their progress. Reconnaissance units, urged forward to seize bridges over the Orne, were halted by rubble-choked streets, another cost of the bombing. Yet, to the astonishment of the Canadians, battered Caennais emerged from the ruins to cheer their liberators and to rejoice that some of them spoke with the Norman accent of the *Canadien*. Civilians also had to begin to put their lives together. "Driving with difficulty down a shattered street," one Canadian recalled, "I saw an old woman sweeping the dust of bombardment from the doorstep of a house of which little more than a doorstep remained. One could either cheer at that blind courage, or weep at its apparent futility."

Canadians had paid a price for Caen's liberation. Casualties—330 dead, 864 wounded—were heavier than D-Day. And, as usual, the victory seemed incomplete. Even the miraculous escape of the church of St. Etienne and the thousands of refugees it sheltered only underlined the needless destruction of the city and its university. At Carpiquet, the Queen's Own had won a bloodless victory five days late but retreating Germans had safely crossed the Orne and savage fights remained.

OPERATION GOODWOOD

With the capture of Caen on July 8 and 9, Montgomery was satisfied—for the moment. His allies were not. The victory had come 33 days late. RAF commanders, already hostile to the arrogant little general, complained they were no closer to the potential airfields south-east of Caen. Above all, the Americans were angry and frustrated. The British might claim that Bradley's 14 divisions faced only 6 German infantry and 2 panzer divisions on their front but, after 10,000 casualties, the American offensive had bogged down at St. Lô. The terrain—a mixture of *bocage* and flooded marshes crossed by narrow causeways—was the real reason but it was easier to blame the British and Canadians for being too slow.

In Washington, American generals shared their worries with SHAEF. All their available infantry divisions were in Normandy or on their way; more would come only in September. Armoured divisions, available in numbers, could serve no purpose until the breakout. The cautious Montgomery was under American pressure. What moved him, though, was not the pressure but news from Ultra. Hitler had renewed his demand for a great armoured assault. As a result, two panzer divisions were slipping westward, away from the British front, and German infantry divisions from farther up the coast were cautiously taking their place.

July 10 was a crucial day. The Americans were exhausted and the Germans were regaining the initiative. A beleaguered Bradley asked for help—ten days to collect supplies and rebuild units for Operation Cobra, the breakout. The British would attack to gain him the time. Three armoured divisions, concentrated as the Germans had never been allowed to be, would squeeze into the narrow bridge-head over the Orne that British and Canadian paratroopers had won a month before. With a route blasted by all the bombers and artillery Montgomery could obtain, they would shatter the German line. The next strategic move was a little vague. In a memo to the corps commander, Montgomery proposed that the attack would "write down" German tank strength, spread panic by sending armoured cars to Falaise and "crack about". At SHAEF, where Allied planners had their own preconceptions, senior officers claimed Operation Goodwood should be the great breakout.

Certainly the prospect seemed tempting. Nowhere in Normandy was the terrain easier for tanks. "Bomber" Harris, overcoming resentment at the waste of his planes at Caen, promised a more precise bombing plan, concentrating on anti-personnel bombing to prevent craters that would impede tanks. Intelligence reported only three to four miles of German defences, manned by infantry and a weak armour reserve.

At dawn on July 18, British bombers delivered the heaviest tonnage of the campaign. Bomb-blasted soil rose in thick clouds of dust. Tanks of the 11th Armoured Division rumbled in a vast tide up the slope, past shaken, shell-shocked German defenders. The Guards and 7th Armoured Divisions followed. Yet British intelligence was wrong: the Germans were not surprised. An extra division of infantry and the toughest of SS panzer division, the 1st *Leibstandarte*

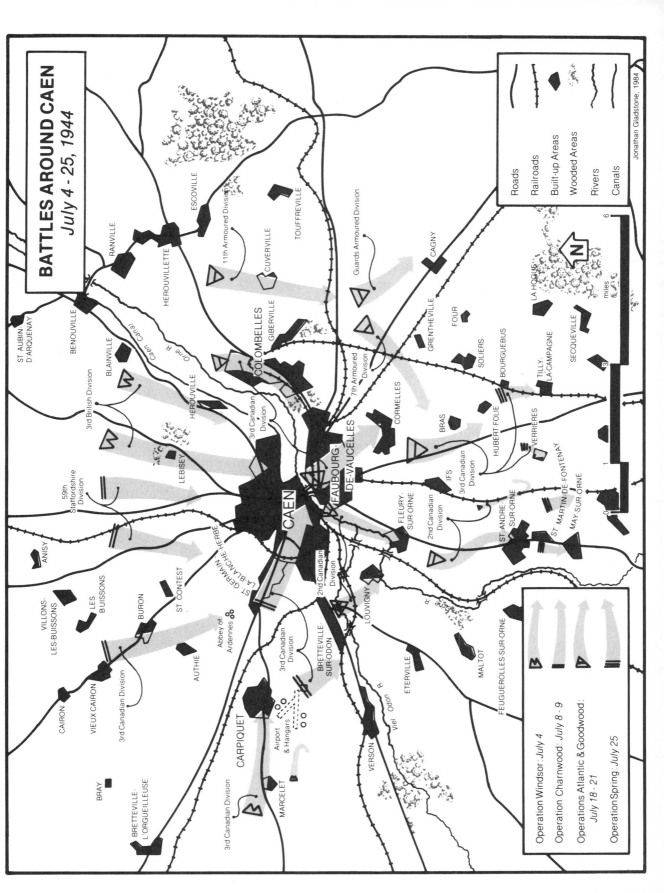

BATTLES AROUND CAEN
July 4 - 25, 1944

Jonathan Gladstone, 1984

Legend:
- Roads
- Railroads
- Built-up Areas
- Wooded Areas
- Rivers
- Canals

N

miles
0   1   3   6

Operations:
- Operation Windsor: July 4
- Operation Charnwood: July 8 - 9
- Operations Atlantic & Goodwood: July 18 - 21
- Operation Spring: July 25

Place names and units:

ST. AUBIN D'ARQUENAY
BENOUVILLE
RANVILLE
ESCOVILLE
HEROUVILLETTE
CUVERVILLE
TOUFFREVILLE
11th Armoured Division
Guards Armoured Division
CAGNY
BLAINVILLE
3rd British Division
HEROUVILLE
Caen Canal
Orne R.
COLOMBELLES
GIBERVILLE
7th Armoured Division
GRENTHEVILLE
FOUR
SOLIERS
BOURGUEBUS
LA HOGUE
SECQUEVILLE
TILLY-LA-CAMPAGNE
LEBISEY
59th Staffordshire Division
CORMELLES
BRAS
HUBERT-FOLIE
VERRIERES
3rd Canadian Division
ANISY
CAEN
FAUBOURG-DE-VAUCELLES
IFS
3rd Canadian Division
FLEURY-SUR-ORNE
2nd Canadian Division
ST. ANDRE-SUR-ORNE
ST. MARTIN-DE-FONTENAY
MAY-SUR-ORNE
VILLONS-LES-BUISSONS
LES BUISSONS
BURON
ST. CONTEST
Abbey of Ardennes
ST. GERMAIN-LA-BLANCHE-HERBE
LA BLANCHE-HERBE
2nd Canadian Division
LOUVIGNY
Orne R.
FEUGUEROLLES-SUR-ORNE
CAIRON
VIEUX CAIRON
3rd Canadian Division
AUTHIE
3rd Canadian Division
BRETTEVILLE-SUR-ODON
ETERVILLE
MALTOT
Odon R.
Viel Odon R.
VERSON
BRAY
BRETTEVILLE-L'ORGUEILLEUSE
MARCELET
CARPIQUET
Airport & Hangars
3rd Canadian Division

Adolf Hitler, had turned three defence lines into five. On Bourguébus Ridge, beyond the bombing and out of range of British guns, rows of 88s, field guns and 272 *Nebelwerfer* or multi-barrelled mortars waited silently. German observers, perched on factory chimneys south of Caen, reported their progress. Even in the shattered villages in front of Bourguébus, defenders had survived the bombing, cleaned off gun-sights and were taking aim.

By noon, the British divisions were in trouble. The Guards Armoured lost 60 tanks as German gunners fought back from their devastated villages. In front of Bourguébus, the 11th Armoured had half its tanks destroyed. As the 88s slaughtered Shermans, Sepp Dietrich, the tough SS tank commander who had once been Hitler's bodyguard and chauffeur, ordered out his Tigers and Panthers. By nightfall, the battered British had barely penetrated beyond the Caen-Vimont railway embankment. Montgomery's first optimistic communiqués, picked up and exaggerated by London newspapers, returned to haunt him.

OPERATION ATLANTIC

On each flank of Operation Goodwood, infantry divisions were to widen the armoured push. Soldiers of the recently constituted II Canadian Corps had the biggest job, crossing the Orne, clearing the industrial suburbs where Caennais had earned their living and shoving south through open country to Bourguébus Ridge itself.

On June 29, General Guy Simonds had finally opened the tactical headquarters of II Canadian Corps at Amblie. British-born, a product of Canadian private schools and the Royal Military College of Canada, Simonds's brilliance made him forge ahead even in the peacetime army. By 1939, he was a major; in 1943, when the 1st Division landed in Sicily, he commanded it as a major-general. At 41, Simonds was a hard, cold, creative commander, much admired and rarely loved. General Crerar, briefly his superior in Italy, had suspected his mental balance. Montgomery regarded him as the one tactical genius the Canadians had produced.

With the arrival of Major-General Charles Foulkes's 2nd Canadian Division in early July, General Simonds's corps was complete. In the lull after Caen, its battalions moved into the line along the Orne to the right of the 3rd Canadian Division. The 2nd Division had Dieppe to avenge; some claimed that it had never quite recovered from the terrible losses. It did not have long to wait for a second test. On July 11, II Canadian Corps became operational. Its share of Goodwood was codenamed Operation Atlantic.

The toughest part of the operation seemed to fall to the veteran 3rd Division. From the British bridgehead, Blackader's 8th Brigade pushed south to Colombelles and the tangled ruins of a steelworks. It was the kind of fighting infantry had to do for themselves, and tanks of the 1st Hussars were of little use. It was fighting that demanded natural leaders—and killed them. The Queen's Own lost men like Rifleman Harry Hawkins, a huge Bren gunner whom men instinctively followed in battle but who had scorned promotion. At Colombelles, the Chaudières were stopped by a big, fortified château. After they pulled back at noon to allow an air attack, they watched as bombs bounced on the flinty soil and flew high in the air. The French Canadians surged forward anyway and took the place. Behind them, battalions had piled up. An impatient Keller pushed the North Shores past and into the steelworks so that his 9th Brigade could fight its way into the Faubourg de Vaucelles. Meanwhile, at Giberville to the east, the Queen's Own Rifles were ripped apart by machine-gun nests. By dark, though, the Toronto men held the village and repelled the inevitable counter-attacks.

In Caen, Foster's brigade waited out the day. With the 3rd Division attack held up by bitter resistance, Simonds ordered a patrol to cross the Orne, with a battalion to follow up. The Regina Rifles slipped a few men across a ruined bridge; by 7:30 p.m., the whole battalion had crossed. The next day, July 19, both the 9th and the 7th Brigades sent battalions forward to the outlying suburbs of Cormelles. After confusion and a brief, painful clash, the men of the 3rd Division finally won their objectives.

For the 2nd Division, Operation Atlantic began more easily. As Goodwood developed to the east, Foulkes's division waited until evening to move forward. By nightfall, the Royal Regiment of Canada had cleared Louvigny, divisional engineers had begun bridging the Orne and Brigadier William Megill's 5th Brigade crossed over to lead next day's attack.

July 19 started well, despite a battlefield snafu that put Le Régiment de Maisonneuve on the line of the artillery barrage and not the proper start line for their attack. Coolly, Colonel H.L. Bisaillon ordered up his reserve companies and the Maisies, in their first battle, fought their way into Fleury-sur-Orne and beyond. To the east, the Black Watch took Ifs. The Canadian objectives were virtually completed. It remained to tidy up the front line.

VERRIERES RIDGE

Operation Goodwood was over. Shattered, burned-out tanks showed what the British armoured divisions had suffered but the two-day carnage had cost fewer than a thousand casualties and the Germans had lost ground, men and tanks. The Shermans could be replaced; the Tigers and their veteran crews could not. Montgomery was satisfied. The 3rd Canadians would relieve the hard-hit 11th

Armoured Division; the lightly scarred 7th Armoured and the 2nd Canadians, at General Simonds's command, would take Verrières and Bourguébus Ridge.

The task certainly seemed necessary, for the 250-foot slope dominated the broad fields south of Caen, hiding tanks and guns that blasted the British armour. It was a vital obstacle on the way south, along Route Nationale 158, to Falaise. On July 20, Brigadier H.A. Young's 6th Brigade, with the Essex Scottish added, moved south of the Orne for the assault. By then, men of the 7th Armoured had already tried an attack, failed and withdrawn beyond the die-straight highway. They and two squadrons of Sherbrooke Fusiliers would back up the assault with artillery fire. For some reason, the infantry was to go forward alone.

On the right, the Queen's Own Cameron Highlanders, a Winnipeg battalion, fought their way into St. André-sur-Orne and stayed, despite ceaseless German shelling and counter-attacks. On the left, Les Fusiliers Mont-Royal had just as difficult a fight for Beauvoir and Troteval farms. It was the South Saskatchewan Regiment, heading down the middle to Verrières, that had the toughest objective and the farthest to go. As the South Sasks advanced, the rain that had threatened all day suddenly burst in a downpour, churning dirt into mud and forcing the circling Typhoons to head for home. Major G.R. Matthews, acting as commanding officer, ordered up every anti-tank weapon he could get as German armour of the dreaded 1st SS rumbled out of the smoke and mist into his ranks. Nothing availed. Matthews and 65 of his men died fighting; 142 were wounded or prisoners. The remnant crawled or ran back through the high grass.

Here they met the battalion of Essex Scottish, exhausted from a sleepless night and an anxious day. Across the fields, behind the retreating Saskatchewan men, came triumphant German tanks and infantry in pursuit. Panic spread. The two leading companies of the Essex dissolved; the rest stayed, fought and somehow stopped the Germans. That night, Brigadier Young reformed the luckless battalion, replaced the colonel and led it back to dig in through the unyielding Norman soil. July 21 dawned with more drenching, demoralizing downpours—weather that delighted the German panzers for it swept the skies of their worst enemy. Again they came, this time shattering the Essex men's frail defences and overrunning both leading companies of the Fusiliers. The Mont-Royals' Troteval Farm fell. Young's brigade faced destruction if the Black Watch, under his command, had not driven forward from Ifs to shore up the line. Verrières and the low, glowering ridge behind it were still held by Germans.

The four days of Operation Atlantic cost Canadians 1965 men, 441 of them killed. Almost a quarter of the dead were Queens' Own Rifles, victims of an endless day of house-to-house fighting. Most of the rest were men of the 2nd Division. The brave, hopeless drive on Verrières had cost the South Sasks 215 men. Panic and the subsequent valiant resistance took 244 men from the Essex Scottish.

An inexperienced division had paid the price of fighting Hitler's toughest veterans. Later, General Foulkes would confess that, for all its years of training, it took two months of action to make his division into a fighting machine. His rejection of the neuro-psychiatric screening that had helped the 3rd Division survive its long ordeal meant that many soldiers of the 2nd were unfit for combat. Among the casualties pouring into Canadian dressing stations behind the line were truckloads of shaking, terrified men who should never have been exposed to battlefield stress.

CONSPIRACY

Predictably, Montgomery took what satisfaction he could from Operation Goodwood. Since much of the battlefield remained in British hands, the shattered tanks could be repaired. Losses were less than the carnage suggested. Above all, three divisions which Rommel had sent to face Bradley at St. Lô had been thrown into the battle south of Caen. Even the futile, costly Canadian attack had forced the Germans to send tanks east across the Orne.

Montgomery's critics were not pacified. Not simply generals and air marshals but the general public had read newspaper accounts of the battle and wondered why three powerful armoured divisions had managed so little. RAF commanders were furious that such small benefit had been gained from their massive bombing. The British chiefs of staff, Eisenhower was advised by Sir Arthur Tedder on July 19, "would support any recommendation which the Supreme Commander might make with reference to Montgomery." Eisenhower would not remove his army commander but the next day he flew to France to share his disappointment and concern. Aware of the British (if not yet the Canadian) reinforcement crisis, the Supreme Commander still plainly wondered whether the Second Army was doing its share.

Yet Montgomery's problems paled beside those of his German counterparts. On July 17, the day before Goodwood, Typhoons near Vimoutiers spotted and strafed a German staff car. From the wreck, near Ste. Foy de Montgommery, passing soldiers hauled the unconscious body of Field-Marshal Rommel.

Three days later, as hot, dusty Canadians waited to attack Verrières, Hitler and his generals leaned over a heavy conference table in their East Prussia headquarters. Suddenly a suitcase bomb underneath exploded. Warned by a codeword, triumphant conspirators in Berlin, Paris and other centres herded Gestapo men and Nazi officials into cells. Then, from East Prussia, came another message. Deaf, stunned, punctured by a hundred fragments, Hitler was still alive—his high, angry voice on the telephone confirmed it. On their third try, the conspirators had failed again. In hours, the regime recovered. Some conspirators committed suicide but most, with their families—4,980 people in all—died slow, terrible deaths at the hands of the Gestapo.

Normandy had been heavy on the conspirators' minds. The impending disaster predicted by von Rundstedt, Rommel and now von Kluge would end any hope of negotiating a peace with the western Allies. Few senior generals, Rommel and von Kluge among them, had been unaware of the plot; Hitler's death would have released them from their oaths of allegiance and Germans from their loyalty. Instead, Hitler was alive, his sense of destiny confirmed, and he was more suspicious than ever of defeatist commanders. No longer would senior officers dare warn of catastrophe or plead for strategic withdrawal. The fate of the conspirators, dying slowly at the end of a length of piano wire as Gestapo cameramen ground out their film, terrorized senior Wehrmacht commanders. At any time they themselves might be implicated.

The end of Operation Goodwood brought little comfort to von Kluge; his mind was on his own fate. German soldiers, reading of the Führer's miraculous escape in *Front und Heimat,* only deepened their traditional contempt for rear-area generals and staff officers. The SS men would fight harder because more of the titled, monocled aristocrats had been swept away. Canadians would feel the consequences.

OPERATION SPRING

By drawing off German armour, Goodwood had made the Americans' Operation Cobra easier. While Dempsey's 14 divisions held 14 German divisions and 600 of the best German tanks on their front, only 9 German divisions faced Omar Bradley's growing army. Yet Cobra could not begin on July 20. The rainstorms that drenched Canadians at Verrières forced delay, first to July 24 and then to July 25. Once again, the British and Canadian front would have to hold the Germans. The task fell to II Canadian Corps.

In three days, from July 21, Simonds's corps headquarters had made its plans for Operation Spring. The brunt fell on the two Canadian infantry divisions. The 3rd would take Tilly-la-Campagne from the veterans of the 1st SS so that tanks of the British 7th Armoured could pour through to seize Cramesnil spur. More Canadians, with tank support, would move on to take Garcelles-Secqueville. On the right, 2nd Division had an even bigger task. First, it would have to clear its own jumping-off point, St. André-sur-Orne to Hubert-Folie. In a second phase, two battalions would rush forward to Verrières and May-sur-Orne and, in a final stage, two more battalions would capture the ridge and the village of Rocquancourt.

The Canadians, in short, must do what had proved impossible for armour and infantry only a few days before. While the 3rd Division tackled the Adolf Hitler Division, the 2nd Division faced the 292nd Infantry Division, backed by tanks, panzer-grenadiers and most of two veteran armoured divisions. Unknown to the Canadians, German snipers, patrols and raiding parties had infiltrated mine shafts and quarries left by Caen's steel industry. As they moved up to battle, Canadians found themselves shot at from every angle by Germans who seemed, quite literally, to vanish into the earth. Strength and morale, both badly needed for the bitter battle ahead, suffered. So did any remote hope of secrecy.

Long before H-hour for the real attack, Les Fusiliers Mont-Royal and the Camerons, backed by Sherbrooke Fusilier tanks, began the fight to capture the start line. This time, the Fusiliers took Troteval Farm. On their right, the Cameron Highlanders fought desperately to win St. André and the adjoining village of St. Martin-de-Fontenay. At 3:30 a.m. on July 25, they reported success. They were wrong. A mine shaft running all the way back to Rocquancourt, undiscovered until days later, let Germans move in and out of the villages at will.

Simonds had scheduled H-Hour at 3:30 a.m. to give his troops at least the cover of night and had called for powerful searchlights, beamed at the clouds as "artificial moonlight", to assist in the advance. But even in daylight, Operation Spring would have been risky. German snipers and patrols were able to penetrate the Canadian lines using secret mine tunnels. Assault battalions, hurrying forward, made noisy, vulnerable targets.

On the 3rd Division front, a single battalion, the North Novas, moved forward in pitch blackness. Minutes later than planned, the searchlights came on. Silhouetted, the Canadians were easy targets for a storm of machine-gun fire. The four assault companies, out of touch with each other and their battalion headquarters, fought their way to the edge of the villages. As dawn broke, Fort Garry tanks were allowed to forget their role in the second phase and go forward to help. Eleven of the 15 tanks were soon burning. So were the carriers and self-propelled anti-tank guns that tried to reach the infantry. After night fell, barely 100 men made their way back. The Stormont, Dundas and Glengarry Highlanders were warned to be ready but the futility was too obvious, and there was no will to advance. Clearly the attack was hopeless.

The 2nd Division had better—and worse—luck. On the right, caught in the confusion of St. André and St. Martin, the Calgary Highlanders were stopped. Losing direction, elements of the battalion made two fruitless assaults on May-sur-Orne. On the left, however, Lieutenant-Colonel John Rockingham used his reserve company to clear the start line before sending the rest of his Royal Hamilton Light Infantry up the slope to Verrières. That meant that the Royal Regiment of Canada, a Toronto unit, and supporting British tanks had a firm base to attack Rocquancourt. In less than a quarter-mile, though, the Royals stopped under devastating German fire. C Company pushed on, only to be wiped out. British tank commanders reported 30 German tanks, lined up like a crowd at a shooting gallery, pulverizing the Canadians.

Into that trap came the Black Watch, an old Montreal regiment that, in peacetime, prided itself on being the most exclusive in the militia. Now it would earn its honour. Since May-sur-Orne, on the flank, was still in German hands, the battalion probably should have stopped. It continued. Near St. Martin, Lieutenant-Colonel Steven Cantlie fell, mortally wounded, and Major F.P. Griffin took the regiment on, past May towards Fontenay. The commander of the supporting tank squadron, Major Walter Harris, in civilian life a Liberal M.P., was wounded and dozens of Black Watch fell. Griffin and the rest struggled on up the ridge to its flat crest. Of 300 men who had started, perhaps 60 reached the top, only to find themselves in a circle of dug-in German tanks and guns. Griffin ordered his men back. Fifteen made it down the ridge; the others fought on until the early afternoon. Griffin's body was found later among those of his men.

Neither its brigade nor the division knew what had befallen the Black Watch. Griffin's jeep and radio were found not far from the start line, knocked out. No tanks had followed the infantry up the ridge; they were diverted to May-sur-Orne as the Maisonneuves, brought up from the rear, tried a third and equally unsuccessful assault. In fact, few higher Canadian commanders seem to have realized how disastrously their infantry battalions had fared during the day. By evening, only Rockingham's battalion was on its objective. Confident that Tilly and May were in Canadian hands, Simonds and his generals made brisk plans for fresh advances on July 26.

The truth became apparent at 6 p.m. when German armour rolled over the ridge at the Royal Hamilton Light Infantry. Tank guns blasted infantry from their hastily dug scrapes in the ground. Three of the four 17-pounder anti-tank guns were knocked out. The fourth, battered and flat-tired, fought on, as did desperate infantrymen with PIATs and grenades. At one point, eight German tanks rolled through the RHLI positions. "From what I saw of Rockingham," an anti-tank gunner recalled, "he feared neither man nor devil, but I believe he put a lot of trust in God, because the rest of us did." That night, patrols stalked German machine-guns. One patrol, trapped for a day behind German lines, returned with an SS man they had caught reading a book.

Long before then, Operation Spring had been called off. Brigadier Young, faced with sending his men on yet another assault on May-sur-Orne, advised against it, and General Foulkes agreed. They found that Simonds had already cancelled further attacks.

The official historian would later calculate that July 25 had been the bloodiest day's work of the war for the Canadian Army, except for Dieppe. With many of their dead and wounded left on German-held soil, and Canadian medical facilities overwhelmed, precise casualty figures for the day could never be compiled, but about 450 Canadians died in Operation Spring and another 1,100 were wounded or prisoners. Rockingham's valiant battalion had lost 200 casualties, 53 of them dead. Its proud boast that none of its soldiers were taken prisoner was not precisely true: two men, wounded on patrol, had insisted on being left behind.

The Black Watch, in its valiant but fatal charge up Verrières Ridge, lost 307 men, 123 of them for ever. Of the 83 men taken prisoner, 21 were wounded. Only at Dieppe did any Canadian battalion suffer such losses in a single day. One of the few survivors was asked why he had gone forward to such certain doom. "I guess," he replied, "that that's what they expected from the Black Watch."

Disasters happen in war. The fate of the Montreal battalion on a hot July day was one tragedy among many, almost forgotten except by those who still grieve and those who burnish the regiment's honours. In 1992, a television series called *The Valour and the Horror* devoted an hour to the battle and launched a public controversy. The producers, armed with a Hollywood image of war, a post-Vietnam contempt for generals and 20/20 hindsight, had no trouble pinning the blame for the setback on the commander of II Canadian Corps, Lieutenant-General Guy Simonds.

No doubt Simonds was a driver, a general who pressed his division commanders to push their brigadiers and colonels. He understood that casualties today could save more lives tomorrow. At Verrières, he overestimated what his raw units and inexperienced commanders could do against German troops who, however weakened, were superbly trained and led. As Colonel Jack English has complained in *The Canadian Army in the Normandy Campaign*, Canadians lacked the tough, remorseless training that was the only possible substitute for learning to fight under fire.

Guy Simonds was no fool. The best general produced by the Canadian army in the war, he was the only one judged a professional by his British and American peers. The producers of *The Valour and the Horror* were too smug in their prejudices to realize that battle is always a confused and confusing affair, with the fog of war hanging thickly over the arena. Simonds did the best he could with what he had; so, too, did the men and officers of the Black Watch.

Captain Alec Christian "mugs up" with his tank crew. The five members of a
Sherman crew fought and lived together in the field, often forming a human
bond that ignored the army's usual concern with rank and status. Christian's
regiment, the Fort Garrys, came from Winnipeg, but westerners seemed to
gravitate to all the armoured regiments. Surviving the Depression seemed to
have made them brilliant "scroungers", and expert mechanics with a little bal-
ing wire and ingenuity. (Author's collection)

Breakfast in a slit trench, July 9, for Corporal Angus Campbell, Privates Freddie Lang and Cliff Peltier and Lance-Corporal Boots Schultz. Eating British rations was one of the heavier costs of Canada's Commonwealth connection. (PA131399/Public Archives Canada)

Canadian soldiers have bitter memories of being bombed and strafed by their own air force during the Normandy campaign, but Allied airpower was the decisive factor in countering the better-equipped German veterans. Pilots like this one, about to take off in his Typhoon from an improvised airfield, made daylight movement enormously costly for German tank columns. (PL40736/Public Archives Canada)

OPPOSITE: The Typhoon's key tank-killing weapon was the rocket, mounted on rails under the aircraft's wings. Small-calibre cannon, here being loaded by Royal Canadian Air Force armourers, provided added firepower when the fighter-bomber swooped on German positions. (PL30936/Public Archives Canada)

Triumphant Canadians return from Carpiquet with one of its young Luftwaffe defenders. Their Universal carrier, blanketed in straw, protects the occupants from rifle bullets but little else. The censor blanked out a shoulder flash to confuse the enemy. (PA132860/Public Archives Canada)

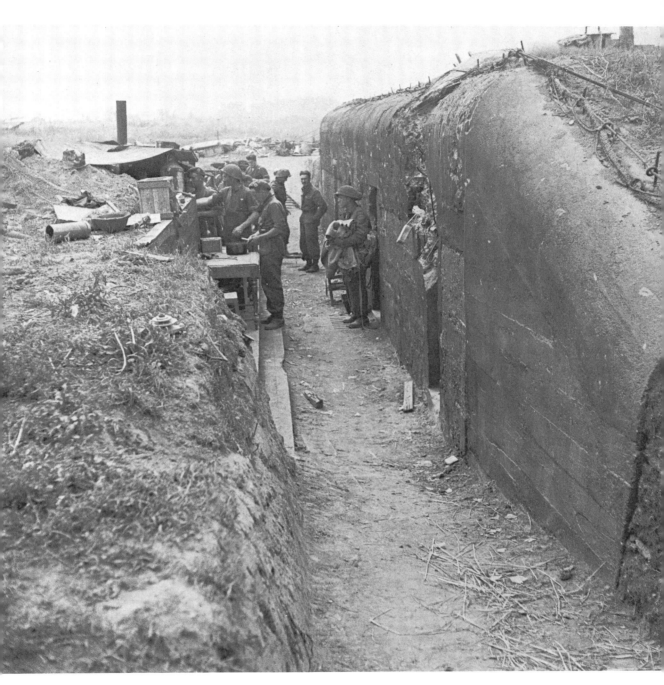

After the capture of Carpiquet, Canadians could finally inspect the huge reinforced-concrete bunkers from which the German defenders had fought with such deadly effectiveness. (PA116513/Public Archives Canada)

Close air support depended on effective ground liaison with the army. Flying Officer J.D. Orr shares danger and hardship as well as a bottle of Calvados with these two members of the Regina Rifles. (PA132857/Public Archives Canada)

Recruiting officers had promised Canada's would-be soldiers that they would be joining a mechanized army but the infantry still walked as much as they rode, laden with the tools of their trade. The high rectangular pouches carry ammunition for the Bren gun, the light machine-gun lugged by the second man over his shoulder. Rifle ammunition was carried in a cotton bandolier on the first soldier's left side. (PA132846/Public Archives Canada)

The crew of "BEBE" pose proudly with their 105mm self-propelled howitzer, an American-made field gun mounted in a tank chassis. The men and their gun belong to the 14th Field Regiment, one of the units that backed up Canadians fighting their way into Caen. (PA132886/Public Archives Canada)

OPPOSITE: Men of the Cameron Highlanders of Ottawa load and fire their Vickers medium machine-gun. A tough, dependable old beast, the Vickers predates the Boer War and was still a champion in the Korean War in the 1950s. Its barrel, encased in a water-filled jacket, boiled water for a soldier's tea while it pumped bullets at an unseen enemy. (PA129037/Public Archives Canada)

Well dug in, with his desk lamp mounted on a stump and his range table in hand, Gunner D.M. Sutton gets ready to plot the range for guns supporting the 3rd Division. The Germans despised much of the Canadian equipment but they were amazed by the speed and accuracy of Canadian artillery fire. (PA132920/Public Archives Canada)

A Canadian crew scrambles out of the way as a big 7.2-inch gun gets ready to fire. Heavy guns like this one were used mainly to knock out German artillery. Handling the huge shells was heavy manual labour and a crew like this earned its pay. (PA132925/Public Archives Canada)

"London Bridge" was one of scores of Bailey bridges hurriedly erected by
Engineers to keep the army moving. This bridge on the Odon helped get the
2nd Canadian Division into action south of Caen as other Canadians pushed
into the shattered city. (PA131392/Public Archives Canada)

OPPOSITE: Private Harry Parker of the Highland Light Infantry, July 9, 1944.
The strain of more than a month of fighting is evident on his face, but for
Parker and his battalion, even tougher fighting lay ahead. (PA131401/Public
Archives Canada)

Sergeant Jack Hickman performs the last and nastiest job of Engineer mine-clearing crews, "lifting" and defusing the mine. Since the Germans were ingenious at thinking up anti-lifting devices, while Canadian generals and colonels demanded faster work, the Royal Canadian Engineers had a job no one envied. (PA132918/Public Archives Canada)

OPPOSITE: For Canadian soldiers, German mines were a nerve-racking danger. An anti-personnel mine could tear off a foot or a leg; anti-tank mines could kill the driver or merely throw a track. Mines, laid in unexpected places, were a major factor in battlefield strain. Mechanized warfare slowed to the pace of brave men like Sapper W.S.S. Grant, probing with his magnetic mine-detector for the tell-tale "beep" which signalled a mine—or just more scrap metal. (PA132856/Public Archives Canada)

Not many battlefield photos catch as much real action as this one. Canadian medium artillery, 5.5-inch guns, blast German positions in Caen as Canadian infantry move south of Caen in the bitter, costly battles of Operation Spring. (PA116516/Public Archives Canada)

The picture may be posed but the Canadian is firing real bullets from his "liberated" German Schmeisser machine pistol. A despatch rider—who probably lent the Schmeisser—crouches a little self-consciously for the photographer. In a real battle, soldiers with any life-expectancy learned to use cover. (PA132727/Public Archives Canada)

OPPOSITE: A Canadian patrol moves cautiously through one of Caen's less devastated streets. The decision to bomb Caen not only did little harm to its German defenders, who had moved to the outskirts; it also made the city almost impassable for Allied vehicles and created scores of hiding-places for snipers. Canadians shared the cost of a military error. (PA116510/Public Archives Canada)

In one of the few miracles of the war, Caen's historic abbey, sheltering many
hundreds of civilian refugees, survived the bombardment almost unscathed.
These women, still uncertain of the blessings of Liberation, stare at Lieutenant
Ken Bell's camera. (PA116290/Public Archives Canada)

French civilians in Caen greet their liberator at the Abbaye aux Hommes. Few could have realized that General Montgomery had been part-author of their city's destruction. While most Normans welcomed the Allied invasion, they were human enough to wish that the blessing might have fallen on some other part of France. (PA132864/Public Archives Canada)

The key leaders of an army in the field are platoon commanders like Lieutenant Alex Miller of Baie Comeau, an officer of Le Régiment de la Chaudière. The average life-span in battle of a platoon commander was a matter of weeks. These were men who made a difference. (PA132867/Public Archives Canada)

General Sir Bernard Montgomery and his temporary American subordinate, Lieutenant-General Omar Bradley, set off for one of the more public duties of generals—distributing medals. This photograph more than hints at their stiff but correct relationship; affection was not exchanged. (PA129133/Public Archives Canada)

Major-Generals R.F.L. Keller and Charles Foulkes endure a publicity photograph with varying degrees of pleasure. Keller's 3rd Division was now a battle-hardened, weary formation; Foulkes's 2nd Division was about to endure its own savage baptism of fire. (PA116519/Public Archives Canada)

South of Caen, the ground was open, pockmarked with little villages turned into fortresses for German troops and tanks. Infantry, as vulnerable as this platoon of the Royal Winnipeg Rifles, had to walk forward much as their fathers had done in the 1914–18 war. Even the weapons were much the same. (PA116528/Public Archives Canada)

South of Vaucelles, two Canadians man a loophole in the wall of a former French barracks. The soldier aiming his rifle has his ammunition in a cotton bandolier slung around his neck. (PA132852/Public Archives Canada)

On July 25, an army photographer caught this Canadian soldier as he moved forward on a night attack. The photograph also shows the limitations of "artificial moonlight" as a device to help the infantry find their way in a night battle. Canadian infantry paid a high price for those lessons to be learned. (PA129124/Public Archives Canada)

Canadian Sherman tanks of the 2nd Armoured Brigade roll up to the Orne, ready for the battles south of Caen. The open country should have been ideal for tanks; instead the high profile of the Sherman made it an easy target for well-placed German 88mm guns. (PA132863/Public Archives Canada)

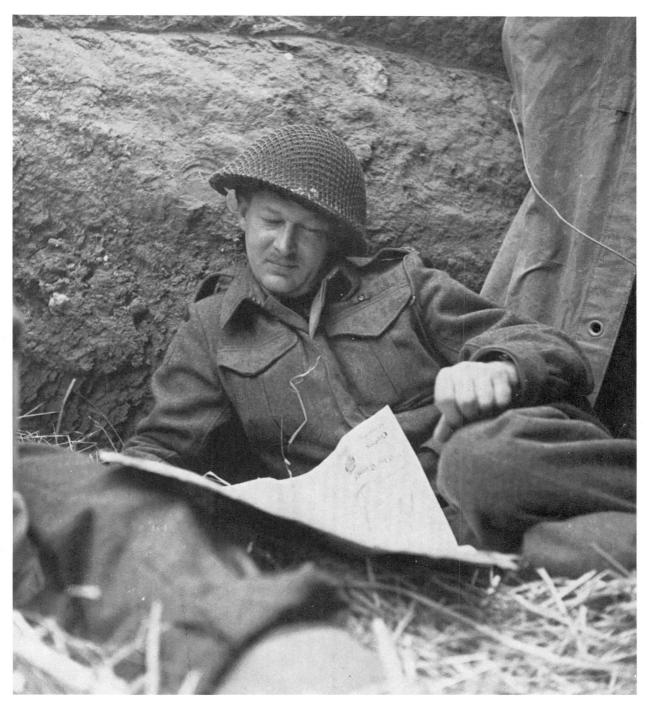

Major Geoff Boone, on the staff of the 8th Brigade and a member of the Queen's Own Rifles, nonchalantly reads a London newspaper while German mortar shells burst in the vicinity. Shelling was an ordeal to be endured as best one could; only the rarest individual could escape the psychological effects entirely. (PA132865/Public Archives Canada)

Hundreds of Canadian women shared in the Normandy campaign as nurses with the Canadian Army or the Royal Canadian Air Force. Army regulations did their best to ensure noncombatant status and to keep them from harm's way. These nurses with No. 10 Canadian General Hospital landed at Arromanches by amphibious truck on July 23. (PA108174/Public Archives Canada)

Official photographers (or their censors) were squeamish about showing the nastier side of an army nurse's work. A boring but acceptable alternative was the old chore of folding bandages. Lieutenants D. Harrison and M. Vincent, both from Manitoba, served with a British hospital. (PA131389/Public Archives Canada)

A hot meal was a vital morale booster and army cooks won grudging praise for their achievements in adversity. A veteran bush cook watches his "dixies" boil while two assistants wait and two others sharpen a carving knife. Canadians prided themselves on living as well as they could in the field. (PA132728/Public Archives Canada)

After the fight for Caen, 3rd Division units like the Regina Rifles got a short, badly needed rest. For these riflemen, it was a chance to shave, pull through the old Lee-Enfield and forget about battles that were still to come. (PA132854/ Public Archives Canada)

Getting clean is a cherished but hopeless dream for a frontline soldier. Farther back, it becomes just a little easier. These men of the Royal Canadian Army Service Corps have improvised a labour-intensive shower bath for Lieutenant George Cooper. (PA132823/Public Archives Canada)

For some Canadians, of course, the people of Normandy were a reminder of home, peace and normal lives that might someday be resumed. For a few days at a rest camp near Caen, these Canadians could share another kind of life in France. (PA132833/Public Archives Canada)

Among the few members of the Canadian Women's Army Corps to serve in Normandy were members of the Canadian Army Show. Enid Powell, Muriel Stuart, Sergeant Linda Tuero and Vera Cartwright hailed from Toronto; Virginia Stansell, on the right, came from Windsor, Ontario. (PA132838/Public Archives Canada)

OPPOSITE: Canadian veterans from the fighting around Caen may have wished that Germans were as absurd as Sgt. Frank Shuster and Sgt. Johnny Wayne suggested. Women in the Canadian Army Show were part of official morale-boosting and a fair replacement for the female impersonators of First World War shows. (PA132839/Public Archives Canada)

IV
The
Falaise Road

After Operation Spring heads rolled. The colonels of the North Novas and the Stormont, Dundas and Glengarry Highlanders (the latter had shown no zeal for throwing his exhausted battalion at Tilly) were removed. So was Brigadier Cunningham. His successor was the redoubtable Colonel Rockingham of the Royal Hamilton Light Infantry.

At SHAEF, complaints about yet another Montgomery failure reached as high as General Eisenhower, though the Supreme Commander grumbled only to British politicians. Montgomery, of course, had an answer when rumours of discontent reached him: by bloodying themselves on some of Hitler's best divisions, the Canadians had kept them from the Americans. As he prepared for the breakout battle, Bradley now mustered an overwhelming 19 divisions and 750 tanks against only 110 German tanks, most of them obsolete, and 9 divisions, some of them mere fragments.

For a month, American troops had practised tank-infantry tactics. Over objections from air force brass, Major-General Elwood Quesada linked his fighter bombers to radio-equipped ground liaison officers. In workshops behind the lines, Sherman tanks were transformed into "Rhinoceroses" with razor-sharp steel "tusks", able to rip through the hedgerows. On July 25, the day of Operation Spring, 1500 Flying Fortresses carpet-bombed the German defences. Cobra, the breakout battle, had begun.

It was bitter going. German survivors manned their weapons and fought back. Bomb craters blocked American tanks. Casualties rose and, by dusk on July 26, Bradley's attack was wilting. A single tough-minded armoured commander drove his men on through the night, and at dawn his combat command cracked the German line. Other armoured units raced through. On July 28, Americans fought their way into Coutances. Two days later they reached the coast at Avranches.

Then, by pre-arrangement, Bradley's army split. The First United States Army kept up the pressure on General Paul Hausser's shaken Germans, but a new Third Army would drive towards Germany. Its commander, Lieutenant-General George S. Patton, in burnished helmet, ivory-handled pistols and gleaming cavalry boots, looked like a stage general. A year earlier, he had lost his command when journalists saw him slapping two shell-shocked soldiers in Sicily. Eisenhower had exploited Patton's formidable fighting reputation by making him commander of the fictional army group poised to land in the Pas de Calais. Now Bradley nervously accepted his former superior; with Patton in charge, no one would have to whip the Third Army forward.

Of course, Montgomery had planned for the breakout. To help the Americans, he sent his British divisions on yet another costly drive into the *bocage*, this time at Mont Pinçon. The outcome of Operation Bluecoat was another four days of frustrating, bloody fighting—but the reserves von Kluge would have sent Hausser were diverted. Next, Montgomery expected, the Germans would withdraw. Nothing else made sense. The Allies must drive eastward to the Seine to force the enemy into one of the most costly operations of war—withdrawal across a river.

Von Kluge and his generals agreed; the sooner they could begin, the more they could save. As early as August 2, they were warned that the Führer had different plans. On August 4, Hitler issued his orders for Operation Lüttich. Von Kluge would assemble 8 of his 9 panzer divisions and launch them at Mortain and Avranches. The Americans would split and crumble.

Demonstrated on a map in East Prussia amid the praise of sycophants, Hitler's plan seemed ingenious. In Normandy, it looked insane. Many of the panzer divisions were battered remnants and assembling them would draw devastating air attacks. In the inevitable disaster, both German armies would be lost. Still, it was the Führer's command. All too aware of his implication in the July 30 assassination plot, von Kluge was in no position to protest. Even Sepp Dietrich, Hitler's former henchman, agreed that protest would be suicidal.

Ultra uncovered the Lüttich plan almost at once. Bradley braced his forces around Mortain, summoned Patton back from Brittany and arranged for air supply if the Third Army should be cut off. Both he and Montgomery, displaying the quality strategists call *coup d'oeil*, saw the opportunity Hitler had made for them. Instead of driving the Germans back to the Seine, they could help them to drive themselves into a narrow, vulnerable pocket. By closing the pocket between Alençon and Falaise, they would trap the two German armies in Normandy.

Of course, that action would demand tough, relentless fighting and sympathetic co-operation among Allied commanders who were beginning to feel less than brotherly love. Montgomery's authority remained until Eisenhower established himself in Europe, but with Bradley now a fellow army-group commander, the relationship was more consultative. Their respective roles in the first two months in Normandy had produced strains made no easier by Montgomery's prickly aloofness and the obvious rapport between Bradley and Eisenhower. With Patton, a robust Anglophobe, now in the field, emotions seemed almost certain to be strained.

FIRST CANADIAN ARMY

On July 23, more than a month after Lieutenant-General Crerar's tactical headquarters were set up in Normandy, the First Canadian Army finally came into being. Never before had so large a formation faced battle under a Canadian commander. For at least some Canadian officers, it was a moment of fierce national pride and the culmination of years of struggle with suspicious Ottawa politicians and indifferent allies.

In the end, it was the British who had made the First Canadian Army possible, by promising to replace the I Canadian Corps, engaged in Italy, with one of their own. The reason, as usual, was practical. While Canadian generals worried about a shortage of volunteers and their politicians feared a conscription crisis, the British simply had no more men at all. By allowing the Canadians their army, the British guaranteed that Canadians would provide the thousands of support troops—drivers, mechanics, cooks and engineers—a mechanized army needed.

The price, of course, was inexperience. Many Canadian generals, like Crerar, had distinguished records as junior officers in the First World War. They had done their best to become professionals in Canada's tiny peacetime army but only in Italy had Canadians had prolonged exposure to war. A proficient administrator, Crerar had been prepared for his army command by a few months of hurried experience in Italy in the winter of 1944. A staff officer, seeking words of praise for Crerar, suggested that he would "never make a bad mistake".

Fortunately, greater qualities were not demanded of Montgomery's army commanders. Like his British counterpart, "Bimbo" Dempsey, Crerar was expected to execute Montgomery's directives. Corps commanders looked after the details. With his army's sector established as the Allies' Channel flank, Crerar's basic task would be straightforward. On the right, he took over Lieutenant-General J. T. Crocker's I British Corps. Crocker's unexpected refusal to obey his Canadian commander's orders ended after a pointed interview with the army commander and Montgomery's blunt advice to both men to show more sense.

By the end of July, all three of the Canadian divisions that formed the core of Crerar's army had landed in Normandy. The last, 4th Armoured Division, was raw even in terms of training in England. Its commander, the 33-year-old Major-General George Kitching, had returned from Italy to replace the veteran Canadian apostle of armoured warfare, Major-General Frank Worthington, but there had been no opportunity for a major shakedown exercise. Battle-scarred veterans looked with mingled pity and contempt at the newcomers with their shiny tanks, fluttering pennants and clean new battledress. They were, snorted a sergeant, ready for a review in Paris but first they would have to get there.

Other newcomers, the 1st Polish Armoured Division, had a different aura. Heads shaven, silent and unsmiling, the Poles were exiles who knew they might never go home. That summer, the Home Army, Poland's resistance movement, had risen in Warsaw as Stalin's armies approached. Then the Red Army politely suspended its advance to allow the Wehrmacht to annihilate their mutual enemy. The Warsaw battle raged on as the Polish exiles reached Normandy. As an armoured division the Poles were as raw as the 4th, though their commander, Major-General Stanislaw Maczek, had won a brief tank battle in 1939 against invading Germans. He and his men were a proud acquisition for Crerar's army.

OPERATION TOTALIZE

At the end of July, II Canadian Corps came under Crerar's command, and the 4th Armoured Division relieved the 3rd Division, now the exhausted survivors of 55 days of uninterrupted front-line service. The last phase of the Normandy campaign began.

For the Canadians, that meant achieving the kind of breakout Bradley's armies had managed near St. Lô. On July 29, Crerar issued his orders: an attack on the Caen-Falaise axis, with Falaise the objective, to be carried out in great strength and with massive air support. The details he left to Simonds.

The Canadians, obeying orders to keep the pressure on, made a series of battalion attacks on the Operation Spring objectives—and paid heavily. On August 1, the Calgary Highlanders launched two successive pre-dawn attacks on Tilly-la-Campagne, only to be driven back. As they withdrew, Brigadier Megill sent them back for a third try, backed this time by a squadron of Fort Garrys. The toll for three failures was 178 casualties, 51 of them fatal. The next night, the Lincoln and Welland Regiment had the same experience. On following nights, other battalions suffered similarly. The Germans learned to sit silently as Canadian patrols probed, then to blast the main body when it approached. At May-sur-Orne on August 5, a painfully rebuilt Black Watch lost 70 men in such a trap, 20 of them dead, 21 others as prisoners.

For Operation Totalize, as the Canadian breakout was christened, Simonds called for more troops—the 51st Highland Division, a British armoured brigade and the Polish armoured division joined the Corps. More troops, Simonds saw, were not enough. To get tanks through the anti-tank screen that had stymied Operation Goodwood, he would use darkness and heavy night bombing by the veteran RAF crews. Another problem, underlined by the 2nd Division's probing attacks, was the vulnerability of the infantry against dug-in German positions. As an ex-gunner, Simonds had a brilliant solution. The field artillery regiments no longer needed the self-propelled guns they had brought ashore on D-Day: the "Priests" would be defrocked, the regiments re-equipped with the dependable 25-pounders and the tank chassis rebuilt to carry infantry. Thus the "Kangaroo", the first armoured personnel carrier, was conceived. In three days a special crew of Canadian electrical and mechanical engineers had stripped and converted 76 Priests. From the navy came complaints that Canadians had been caught cutting plate steel from beached landing craft. The purpose was to cover empty gun compartments.

Simonds's plan for Totalize was complex and demanding. In the first phase, the 2nd Canadian and 51st Highland Divisions, led by tank brigades, specialized assault armour, engineers and anti-tank artillery, would roll forward at night in separate, regiment-sized columns. In each, an infantry battalion would ride in the new armoured carriers. Drivers would keep direction by following a radio beam, by searchlights bounced off low cloud and by steady tracer fire from Bofors light anti-aircraft guns posted on the flanks. While the armoured columns rolled forward three or four miles to seize their objectives, other infantry units would secure closer objectives already blasted by Harris's bombers. Once the 2nd Division had broken into the German line, the Poles and two more Canadian divisions, the 3rd and the 4th Armoured, would push through the gap and race to far deeper objectives. In a third and final phase, the Canadian and Polish armoured divisions would drive on to Falaise.

Ambitious as Simonds's plan was, it required time. Troops needed at least a week to train in the new tactics. Despite earlier breezy promises of aid, Sir Arthur Harris had a legitimate horror of being asked to bomb targets so close to the Canadian lines at night. His objections faded when his liaison officers returned convinced that targets could be marked by coloured pyrotechnics from Canadian guns. On top of that, both Hitler and the Americans imposed changes on the plan. To get panzer divisions for Operation Lüttich, Hitler's planned counter-attack, von Kluge pulled the 1st SS from the Canadian front, substituting the 89th Division, so Simonds promptly lengthened the run of each of his first two phases. As for the Americans, Patton's bold race south and east pressured the Canadians to speed up their attack, as did the beginning of Lüttich on August 7 and the costly triumph of the British 43rd Division in capturing Mont Pinçon.

All day on August 7, Canadian, British and Polish tanks and vehicles rumbled into place in the fields and orchards before Verrières Ridge. Twenty-six years before, as Crerar reminded his generals, Canadians at Amiens had helped win a smashing victory which General Ludendorff later called "a black day for the German Armies". August 8, 1944, he hoped, would be "an even blacker day". More relevant to the waiting soldiers, he suggested that victory might mean a quick end to the war.

THE BREAK-IN

Before 11 p.m. on August 7, waiting troops heard the low, ominous rumble of approaching bombers. Over a thousand came, dumping 3,462 tons of explosives. Batteries of 88s, left behind by the panzer divisions, downed ten of the big planes but it was dust and smoke, obliterating marker shells, that stopped the bombing before it was two-thirds done. Harris's orders were strict. To the Canadians, deafened but exhilarated by the devastation, the early halt hardly mattered. At 11:30, the armour and infantry moved forward, with 2nd Division's columns to the west of the Caen-Falaise road, the Highland Division and 33rd British Armoured Brigade to the east.

Veteran armoured officers feared any major movement at night. Peering through a narrow slit or a glass periscope, tank drivers could see little at the best of times. Crew commanders, perched in the turret, were hardly better off. No one had expected the clouds of dust and smoke, boiled up by the bombing and now thickened as tanks followed tanks through the murk, bumping over ditches and lanes, occasionally colliding. The Germans, recovering from their terrible ordeal, opened fire. In darkness, the sudden flames of a burning tank or carrier seemed more terrifying than ever.

Each of the four Canadian columns lost its way. Instead of passing west of Rocquancourt, the Royal Regiment went east of it, and the Royal Hamilton Light Infantry seemed to have driven through the strongpoint as the German garrison hid. The colonel of the Fort Garrys jumped from his tank to redirect a rampaging squadron of the Sherbrooke Fusiliers—heading straight across the Canadian front. The unhappy Essex Scottish got completely lost. By the time it was reorganized, the battalion had suffered heavy casualties. Yet, by noon, both attacking divisions were on or close to their objectives.

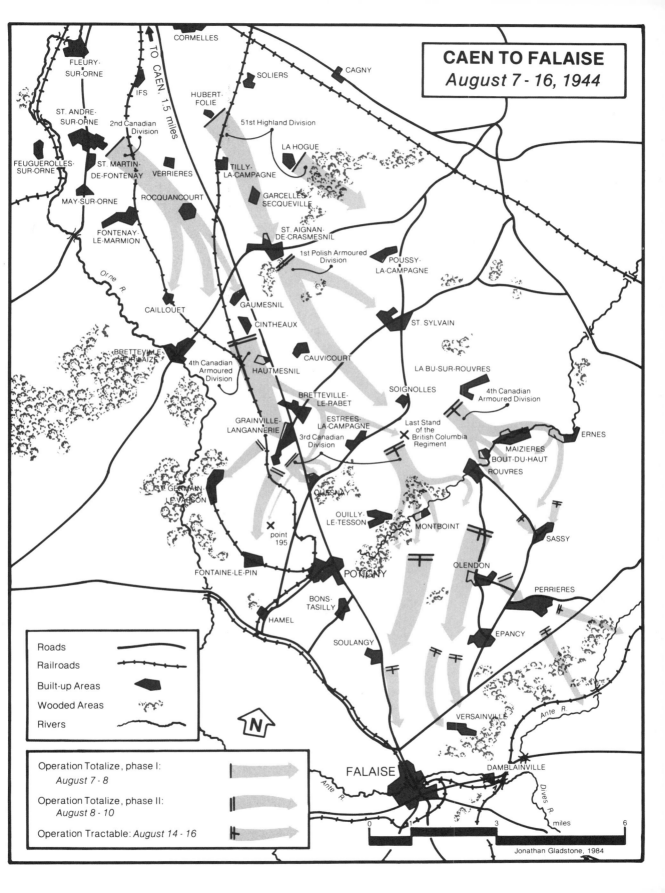

CAEN TO FALAISE
August 7 - 16, 1944

CORMELLES

FLEURY-SUR-ORNE

TO CAEN, 1.5 miles

IFS

SOLIERS

CAGNY

HUBERT-FOLIE

ST. ANDRE-SUR-ORNE

2nd Canadian Division

51st Highland Division

LA HOGUE

FEUGEROLLES-SUR-ORNE

ST. MARTIN-DE-FONTENAY

VERRIERES

TILLY-LA-CAMPAGNE

MAY-SUR-ORNE

ROCQUANCOURT

GARCELLES-SECQUEVILLE

FONTENAY-LE-MARMION

ST. AIGNAN-DE-CRASMESNIL

1st Polish Armoured Division

POUSSY-LA-CAMPAGNE

Orne R.

CAILLOUET

GAUMESNIL

CINTHEAUX

ST. SYLVAIN

CAUVICOURT

LA BU-SUR-ROUVRES

BRETTEVILLE-SUR-LAIZE

4th Canadian Armoured Division

HAUTMESNIL

SOIGNOLLES

4th Canadian Armoured Division

ERNES

BRETTEVILLE-LE-RABET

ESTREES-LA-CAMPAGNE

Last Stand of the British Columbia Regiment

MAIZIERES

GRAINVILLE-LANGANNERIE

3rd Canadian Division

BOUT-DU-HAUT

ST. GERMAIN-LE-VASSON

QUESNAY

ROUVRES

point 195

OUILLY-LE-TESSON

MONTBOINT

SASSY

FONTAINE-LE-PIN

OLENDON

POTIGNY

PERRIERES

BONS-TASILLY

HAMEL

EPANCY

SOULANGY

Legend

Roads	
Railroads	
Built-up Areas	
Wooded Areas	
Rivers	

N

VERSAINVILLE

Ante R.

Operation Totalize, phase I:
August 7 - 8

Operation Totalize, phase II:
August 8 - 10

Operation Tractable: *August 14 - 16*

FALAISE

Ante R.

DAMBLAINVILLE

Dives R.

0   1   3   miles   6

Jonathan Gladstone, 1984

Behind them, Brigadier Young's 6th Brigade had been left to capture the line of mining villages that had defied Canadians for so long. On the left, Colonel Fred Clift's South Sasks finally had an easy battle as the bomb-dazed defenders of Rocquancourt gave up. On the right, where few bombs had fallen, Les Fusiliers Mont-Royal needed two bloody assaults and help from flamethrowing Crocodiles to take May-sur-Orne. The Queen's Own Cameron Highlanders lost two successive commanding officers and a third of their battle strength, but they seized Fontenay and then fought off a German tank-led counter-attack.

Phase One had succeeded on both flanks, and Simonds's daring innovations were fully justified. In their "Kangaroos", 4th Brigade lost 7 dead and 56 wounded, while Young's brigade, with four battalions on foot in the open, lost 68 dead and 192 wounded, almost half of them from the Camerons.

With two German lines breached, Phase Two could begin. On paper, it seemed easy enough. In practice, moving thousands of tracked and wheeled vehicles south through the incredible confusion of a battlefield demanded luck and experience. The Poles and the 4th Canadians had neither. Traffic jams, dense dust clouds hanging in the hot summer air, sniping and occasional bitter fighting on the slopes of Verrières Ridge, where the 2nd Division did its unfinished business, all slowed Kitching's 4th Armoured Division. Impassioned commands to keep moving made no difference.

To give momentum to his second phase, Simonds had called on the U.S. Army Air Force for the kind of day bombing that had helped Bradley's men at St. Lô. The Americans obliged. Soon after 1 p.m., 678 bombers from the U.S. 8th Air Force roared over the Canadian lines. Again, German anti-aircraft guns took their toll. Nine Fortresses fell, one of them jettisoning its bombs over Canadian troops and leading others to follow suit. Another twelve-plane group also bombed short, blasting Canadian gun positions and the vehicles of Polish and Canadian divisions hurrying south. The accident was painful and demoralizing. One Canadian officer wrote that he "looked up to see a wave of Flying Fortresses appear. The men had started to cheer them on when the cheers died in their throats—the bomb-bay doors were opening and from them bombs were falling …falling on the crossroads I had just left. 'My God,' I said to my men, 'there goes the General.'" And in fact General Keller was badly wounded. Three hundred others, Poles and Canadians, lay dead or wounded. Two companies of the North Shore Regiment were wiped out and the 4th Medium, a French-Canadian artillery regiment supporting the Poles, lost half of its sixteen guns.

Yet the real nemesis for Operation Totalize was now racing up the Falaise road in his customary command vehicle, a motorcycle. Kurt Meyer's 12th SS had been west of the Orne and heading for Operation Lüttich when clouds of dust on

August 6 and 7 gave notice of Simonds's attack. Now, as his battle groups deployed near Cintheaux, Meyer headed north. He was appalled to find, for the first time in his experience, German soldiers fleeing a battlefield. He stopped them. At pistol-point, he forced frightened Luftwaffe gunners to turn their anti-aircraft 88s back into anti-tank guns and mobilize for the Canadian attack. The lull between phases was his chance.

Thanks to Meyer and his seasoned battle groups, the slow-moving, uncertain assault of the two armoured divisions made little headway. By evening, the Argyll and Sutherland Highlanders, a Hamilton regiment, and the South Alberta Regiment, Kitching's reconnaissance unit, had fought their way almost to the great quarry at Hautmesnil. On the right, the 2nd Division took Bretteville-sur-Laize and then, under concentrated fire from the Luftwaffe flak batteries, withdrew from the ruins. By dusk, Phase Two of Operation Totalize was running out of steam.

TRAGEDY ON A NAMELESS HILL

With all of his divisions committed, Simonds could do little but demand a steady push through the night. Later, he was furious to discover that most of the armoured regiments of the 4th Division simply "harboured" as darkness fell, as they invariably had during exercises in England. Some even withdrew to find a safer shelter. Brigadier E. L. Booth did what he could to keep up the momentum. "Halpenny Force", named for the Guards' commanding officer, Lieutenant-Colonel W. W. Halpenny, and composed of the tanks of the Canadian Grenadier Guards and infantry of the Lake Superior Regiment, was commanded to move on to Bretteville-le-Rabet. Lieutenant-Colonel D.G. Worthington's British Columbia Regiment, with infantry from northern Ontario's Algonquin Regiment riding on its tanks, would advance through the darkness to take high ground south-west of Quesnay Wood, crossing the main Falaise road.

Worthington's force set off in pitch darkness early on August 9, passed Colonel Halpenny's men, and rumbled on, undistracted by occasional bursts of fire. Anyone who has ever hiked across country at night will understand what followed. Instead of swinging right in front of Quesnay, most of the column headed east of Estrées-la-Campagne, bumped over a lateral road and halted as day broke in the midst of an open field surrounded by hedges and thick clumps of trees. Though upset that one of his squadrons and a company of Algonquins was missing (it had peeled off to the north-east and headed into the Polish lines) Worthington was certain that he had reached his objective.

Instead he was almost four miles away—a problem compounded when the force mistakenly transmitted its location as a point close to Caen. A German officer, astonished to see an enemy tank regiment parked in a field, was taken prisoner. In fact, Worthington's night ride had taken him almost into the guns of Battle Group Wünsche, the main remaining force of Meyer's 12th SS. Caught in the open field, without cover or time to dig in, the Algonquins and the British Columbians fought a hopeless day-long battle. Since no one at Brigadier Booth's headquarters could find them, no help came. A couple of low-flying Typhoons gave welcome support but made no report. Even when eight surviving tanks broke out, no accurate location was reported. By dusk, according to later testimony from a British staff officer with the column, even the wounded were fighting. Worthington ordered all who could to escape in the darkness. Then, after a day of cool leadership, he died under a stray mortar bomb.

This lonely fight on a nameless hill cost the B.C. regiment 47 tanks, 40 dead, 34 prisoners and 38 wounded. Their partners, the Algonquins, lost 128 men, 45 of them dead. Both regiments lost their colonels. Though the battle was an epic of courage and sacrifice, it yielded no redeeming tactical gains. Caught by relentless German defenders, neither Poles nor Canadians gained ground on August 9. That night, however, a brilliantly led attack by Lieutenant-Colonel J. D. Stewart carried the Argyll and Sutherlands to both the hills that Halpenny and Worthington had been ordered to take. As German artillery blasted the Canadian infantry in furious vengeance, the 3rd Division, backed by the 2nd Armoured Brigade, tried to regain the initiative by taking Quesnay Wood and forcing a way to the Laison River.

The attack, by 8th Brigade, was spearheaded by Colonel Jock Spragge's Queen's Own Rifles and the North Shores. The unsuspecting Canadians walked into a wall of Hitler Youth, backed by all the guns Kurt Meyer could muster on the heights beyond the Laison River. Against youngsters eager to die for the Fatherland, the Queen's Own men were in trouble. The Germans held their fire until the Canadians were on the edge of the woods, then blasted them. In the leading company every officer and sergeant fell, and a brand-new corporal, Nick Zamaria, took command. On their front, the North Shores, cut to three companies after the bombing fatalities caused by the U.S. 8th Air Force, lost their colonel, Don Buell, and as many men as the Queen's Own. The battle of Quesnay Wood cost Canadians 44 killed and 121 wounded.

Operation Totalize had broken down. Early on August 11 an angry, frustrated Guy Simonds called off further attacks, lined up the infantry divisions to hold the new front and urgently started to make new plans.

OPERATION TRACTABLE

On August 7, von Kluge's Operation Lüttich began. One day later it ended.

Instead of eight panzer divisions, he had mustered only four. Fresh divisions, summoned from southern France, were pulverized from the air. By August 12, backed by SS generals whom he earlier had despised, the German field-marshal pleaded with Hitler for the right to withdraw. By afternoon, Allied pilots saw the long columns of German tanks, vehicles and horse-drawn wagons moving east, not west. The targets were easy and irresistible. What Germans would call the "Cauldron" was beginning to glow with the fires of destruction.

It was more urgent than ever for the Allies to close the gap. On August 10, Montgomery ordered Crerar to swing east of Falaise and drive for Trun on the River Dives. The failure of Totalize showed that that was easier said than done. The Germans were not fools and, whatever Hitler's dark suspicions, von Kluge was a shrewd defensive strategist who had not given up. For Simonds, the challenge was to find some new way of smashing the German line—and quickly!

The result was a scheme few coffee-table strategists would use, even in desperation: Simonds resolved to line up his masses of armour in two huge blocks, mask the flanks by bombing and smokescreens, and set the whole array charging across the Norman countryside in broad daylight in a drive for death or glory. Two columns, one based on the 4th Armoured, the other on the 3rd Division and the veteran 2nd Armoured Brigade, would be the Canadians' best shot at smashing through to Falaise. The key was speed, surprise and enough daylight to avoid the wasteful confusion of Totalize. This was Operation Tractable. It would begin on August 14.

For support, Simonds called on every gun in the army and on RAF Bomber Command. (One raid by the Americans had been enough.) For speed, and to safeguard the secrecy of the operation, he issued no written orders. Instead, he summoned every senior officer to his headquarters: armoured commanders, he insisted, must drive their units to the limit and beyond. One unfortunate officer raced back from the meeting, lost his way and blundered into the German lines. Notes and map traces for the attack were found on his dead body. The defenders, two Wehrmacht divisions fresh from Norway, were warned.

To get ready took a full twenty-four hours and involved almost every fighting unit in the Corps. Moving more like veterans now, the Canadians managed it—barely. Whole fields were filled with tanks, Flails, Kangaroos, carriers and guns, waiting in long, dense columns. Soldiers sat smoking, chatting nervously in the warm, still morning. There was a smell of wheat in the air.

At 11:42 a.m., the shout came: "Move now!" Lead tanks and Flails roared into life and rolled forward. Gun crews leaped to their posts. Fighter bombers screamed over the horizon to slam pre-set targets. In the windless summer air, dense clouds of dust joined the smoke shrouding the surging columns. Sweating drivers aimed their vehicles at the faint red ball of the distant sun. Some careered wildly out of line, prodded by some private sense of direction.

Simonds pointed the columns wide of Quesnay Wood, waiting for 769 of Harris's bombers to blast its defenders. On schedule, they did so, dumping 3,723 tons of explosive into the dust clouds. Sadly, the accident Harris hoped to avoid happened, as 77 bombers, assuming the yellow markers were targets, not friends, unloaded their bombs on the Canadian rear. In the hurry, no one had questioned whether Harris's crews knew that yellow was the Allies' daytime recognition signal, as it had been since D-Day, and as nocturnal animals, the bombers had never seen it. The mistake cost 165 Canadian and Polish lives. As the history of the Queen's Own Rifles noted, "C and D Companies should have been right in the centre of the carnage but a Military Policeman on point duty had split the Queen's Own convoy at a crossroad to let another convoy through." As a result, the Queen's Own lost only two men. Among the near-victims sheltering in Simonds's armoured car was Air Marshal Sir Arthur Coningham, a senior RAF commander. Short bombing did not occur again.

German defenders also blasted the Canadians, pumping 88mm shells into the packed columns. The steel tornado roared on, drivers almost unaware of losses hidden by the dust and smoke. Among the casualties were the headquarters tanks of the 4th Armoured Brigade. Brigadier Booth, his leg almost torn off by a German shell, died before help could reach him.

Then came the Laison River. Staff officers had ignored the little creek; its steep muddy banks hardly showed on maps or air photos. Now tanks poured over its banks only to be hopelessly mired. Two squadrons of the 1st Hussars were stuck, waiting for the Germans to find their range. To the right, troopers of the Fort Garrys jumped from their tanks and manhandled tree trunks—chopped by the barrage of 88 shells—into the stream. Infantry poured out of their Kangaroos, waded across the river and stormed into the villages of Rouvres and Montboint. The Wasps, new carrier-borne flamethrowers, helped. Finally, on a few forgotten bridges, the tank squadrons began to pour over the Laison. Groups of infantry, often a mixture of two or three battalions, hurried after. For once, German resistance collapsed. Hundreds of field-grey soldiers now wanted only to surrender.

The next day the fighting changed. Again, Kurt Meyer's tiny remnant of a division made the difference. His fifteen remaining tanks led a pre-dawn counter-attack on the 1st Hussars. Young panzer-grenadiers seemed bent as ever on dying. The 4th Armoured Brigade's three regiments fought bravely but no commander gave them direction. Hungry, tired men of the Canadian Scottish suffered their worst losses since the D-Day landing as the price of taking a key hill on the Falaise road. On their left, the Grenadier Guards and a rebuilt British Columbia Regiment got close to Versainville but German anti-tank gunners drove them back. Only on the third day did the Regina Rifles take and hold the village. By then, there were fresh orders.

THE FALAISE GAP

On August 14, Patton's armoured spearhead had fought its way to Argentan and stopped. The Americans had reached the inter-army boundary, and Bradley's orders were clear. To push on risked a blind clash with the Canadians. Patton, grasping the opportunity, pleaded for orders to continue. "Let me go on to Falaise," he blustered, "and we'll drive the British into the sea for another Dunkirk." His instinct was right. Beyond Falaise, Simonds's four weary divisions faced eighteen miles of tough terrain before they could plug the gap. Patton's exhilarated divisions would make the difference. Bradley insisted: Paris was the objective. Eisenhower agreed. Montgomery said nothing. With Bradley's approval, Patton left enough troops to hold the "shoulder" at Argentan and raced eastward to Paris and the Seine. From Montgomery came only insistent orders to Crerar: the 4th Armoured and the Poles must close the gap between Trun and Chambois "at all costs and as quickly as possible".

On August 16, braving wild traffic snarls, Simonds shuffled his divisions, set the 2nd to capture Falaise from the west and prepared to launch his armoured formations in a desperate bid to bar the German retreat. Two raw divisions, still learning from their first two weeks of fighting, would face the hardbitten survivors of two superb German armies bent on escape across the wooded, rolling valley of the Dives River.

By then, even Hitler grudgingly approved retreat. The day before, disasters had rained on him, from collapse on the Russian Front to an American landing in the south of France. Word that von Kluge had vanished persuaded the Führer that his general had deserted, was perhaps even selling his army to the Allies. Instead, von Kluge had been strafed and nearly killed by Allied fighters. Next evening, Field-Marshal Walter Model unexpectedly arrived to take over. Von Kluge was through. The following day, on a plane to Metz, he wrote a farewell letter to Hitler, pleading his loyalty and the need for Germany to make peace. Then the unhappy general swallowed poison and died.

Model was now free to try to save the two beaten German armies. The 2nd SS Panzer Corps, which had already escaped the "Cauldron", was ordered back to smash the Canadians. A weaker panzer corps could hold off the Americans who had unaccountably halted. It would take three days, Model claimed, to save the

Seventh Army; by August 18, pressed by British and American forces, it was already safely east of the Orne.

Its ordeal was indescribable. Day and night, long columns of vehicles, two abreast, clogged the roads. Above, Allied fighter-bombers logged thousands of sorties. Columns of smoke rose from burned-out tanks and petrol tankers. Abandoned guns, wagons and the stinking carcasses of thousands of horses littered the route. Still the Germans fought and moved. General Hausser, badly wounded, reached safety on the back of a tank after three agonizing days. Colonels and generals, leading battle groups of a few hundred men loaded in the remaining tanks and armoured half-tracks, burned with determination to break through. The more half-hearted Germans hid, surrendered or were driven forward like sheep by ruthless SS men.

On August 17, Canadians of the 2nd Division took Falaise, though it was another day before Les Fusiliers Mont-Royal had killed the last SS holdouts. Except for its castle, the ancient Norman town was in utter ruins. To the east, the 4th Armoured and the Poles began fighting their way across the gap with what, at headquarters, seemed exasperating slowness. On August 18, after four and a half days of missed opportunity, two American divisions and a Free French division began fighting north towards Chambois, against resistance grown enormously stronger in the interval. That morning, after a night-long wait to get organized, the Canadian Grenadier Guards and the Lake Superior Regiment assaulted Trun—to find it unoccupied.

The Canadians pushed to the highway that linked Falaise, Trun and Chambois, developing a first line of resistance against retreating Germans. Meanwhile, General Maczek's Poles struggled cross-country, sometimes lost in the dense woods and too often strafed by Allied fighters and bombers, to form both a second line of resistance and a shield against Model's developing counter-attack. To prevent a clash with the Americans, Crerar sent a liaison officer to First U.S. Army headquarters. There, the astonished Canadian officer was told that he was not wanted, and he duly returned. The Americans would deal only with Montgomery.

MACZUGA AND DIVES

Once the Poles and Canadians were launched into the maelstrom of the gap, there was little Simonds or his divisional commanders seemed able to do to help. Like the remnants of twenty shattered German divisions, Canadian and Polish tank regiments and infantry battalions were destined to fight their own desperate battles.

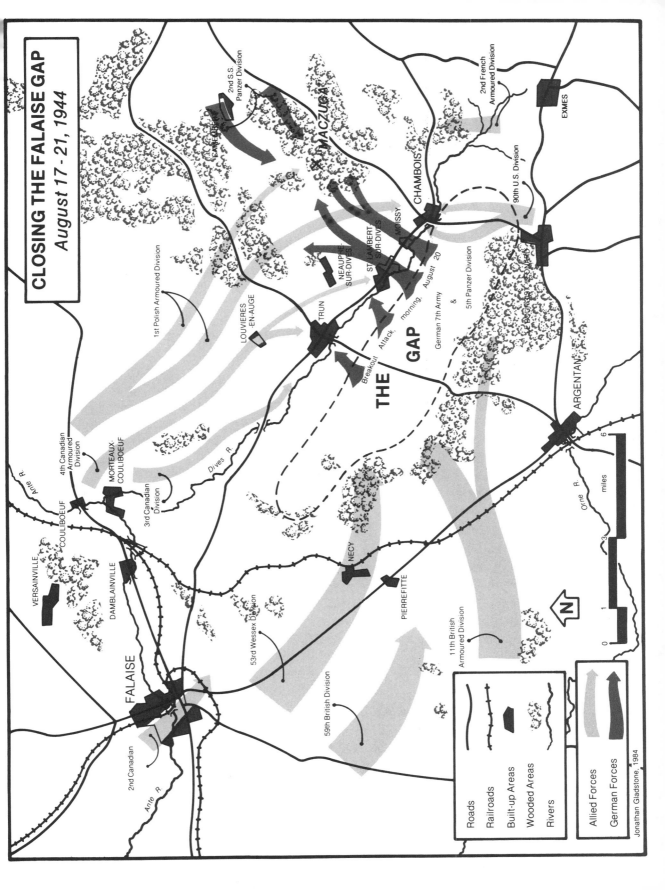

CLOSING THE FALAISE GAP
August 17 - 21, 1944

2nd S.S. Panzer Division

2nd French Armoured Division

EXMES

CHAMBOIS

XV MACZUGA

CAMEMBERT

90th U.S. Division

1st Polish Armoured Division

NEAUPHE-SUR-DIVES

ST. LAMBERT SUR-DIVS.

MOISSY

LOUVIERES-EN-AUGE

TRUN

August 20

5th Panzer Division

Attack, morning,

German 7th Army &

2nd Panzer Division

4th Canadian Armoured Division

Breakout

THE GAP

MORTEAUX-COULIBOEUF

ARGENTAN

Dives R.

3rd Canadian Division

COULIBOEUF

Ante R.

VERSAINVILLE

DAMBLAINVILLE

Orne R.

NECY

53rd Wessex Division

PIERREFITTE

miles

11th British Armoured Division

0   1   3   6

FALAISE

59th British Division

2nd Canadian

Ante R.

N

Roads

Railroads

Built-up Areas

Wooded Areas

Rivers

Allied Forces

German Forces

Jonathan Gladstone, 1984

Full of anguished awareness that Home Army comrades were fighting and dying in the distant Warsaw uprising, the Poles launched their advance even before the pre-dawn H-Hour on August 18. Moving at right angles to the two German-held roads that led out of the pocket to Vimoutiers, one column found itself far to the east, at Les Champeaux. On the way, Poles had watched incredulously as German traffic controllers stopped the flow to let them past. Even the error had benefits, as the Poles caught up with and destroyed part of a German panzer division some of them had seen in far different circumstances in Poland five years before.

On August 19, General Maczek split his division. A third of it, spearheaded by armoured and reconnaissance regiments, drove cross-country towards Chambois. That evening, as the leading squadron fought its way into the town, shouted orders sent men scattering to repel a sudden counter-attack. Then, white flags and familiar rounded khaki helmets appeared. The Poles and the men of the 90th U.S. Division had finally met. The Falaise Gap was closed.

Most of the Polish division, two tank regiments and three infantry battalions, headed straight for a long wooded ridge that commanded the Trun-Vimoutiers road and much of the surrounding country. Maczek had stabbed the point on his map and christened the position Maczuga, Polish for mace, the club-like medieval weapon. There, while Bor-Komorowski's Home Army planned its final despairing breakout in Warsaw, Maczek's men would exact their own terrible vengeance from the Germans. Exhausted after three sleepless nights and days, the Poles waited and dozed in the sunshine.

To the west, the Canadians had also driven a corridor down the highway from Falaise to Trun and Chambois. As they went, battalions from the 9th and 10th Brigades peeled off and dug in along the Dives River. Gunner officers contacted their batteries, preparing for furious German assaults. South from Trun, Major D. V. Currie led his squadron from the South Alberta Regiment, and a company from the Argyll and Sutherlands. It was a familiar partnership but a pitifully meagre force for so historic a role. At St. Lambert, the Germans controlling the last unbroken road to Vimoutiers had to fight—and they did. So did Currie's men, for six savage hours. By afternoon two more infantry companies had joined them, but the Canadians, outnumbered and enveloped, could claim only half the town.

Between them, Poles, Canadians and Americans had closed the Falaise gap. Model's plans had come too late. Swiftly, he switched his orders. Inside the circle, a paratroop general, Eugen Meindl, orchestrated the remaining tanks and battle groups; outside, General Heinrich Eberbach reorganized the 2nd SS Panzer Corps and sent it down the Vimoutiers road. Caught in the middle, the

Canadians and Poles would be smashed. Rain late on August 19 was more than an omen—it warned that weather would ground the fighter-bombers on August 20. The climax of the Normandy campaign had come. It would be a soldiers' battle.

CRISIS IN THE GAP

As with many great moments of history, only a handful of men were involved. At Maczuga, Colonel Stanislaw Koszutski's regiments mustered 80 tanks, perhaps 1600 men. Currie, cut off at St. Lambert, counted just over 200. The German battle groups converging on the battle numbered a few thousand, not counting the other thousands simply struggling to escape or, if SS battle police were elsewhere, to surrender.

Throughout August 20—a Sunday, as a few soldiers noted—waves of Germans poured forward wherever Canadians had taken a stand. At Trun, men of the Lincoln and Welland Regiment and machine-gunners from the New Brunswick Rangers began to sicken at their own slaughter. To the south, Currie's plight grew more urgent. His feeble anti-tank weapons proved no match for the awesome Tigers. Finally, he called for artillery support, remembering too late that the big 5.5-inch shells from the medium guns within range could demolish his few remaining Shermans. Luckily, it was only Germans they hit.

While Germans could still batter their way through St. Lambert or slip past American and Canadian battalions at Trun and Chambois, they could not escape Maczuga. From the afternoon of August 19, the Polish position was the real plug in the bottle. Captain Pierre Sévigny, linking his 4th Medium Regiment with the Poles, grew dismayed at the devastation guns, tanks and infantry wreaked on the narrow Vimoutiers road. Then, as night came without fresh supplies of ammunition, petrol and food or transport to remove casualties and prisoners, the Poles suddenly realized their own isolation and danger. The long cross-country drive had left them with no fuel to move forward or back. Ammunition was running low. By now, German guns were blasting the hill. All day on August 20, Meindl's crack paratroopers and Eberbach's panzers kept up a relentless pressure. Without protective Typhoons, the Poles risked and lost dozens of their vulnerable Shermans. By nightfall, almost a third of the Poles were dead or wounded. Their wounded commander, Colonel Koszutski, summoned the few remaining officers, including Sévigny, for a last conference. "Tonight," he concluded dramatically, "we die."

The night, in fact, was quiet. Driven into a narrow perimeter, the Poles could not stop the retreating Germans and they were left alone. At dawn, it was different. German infantry poured up the hill in a suicidal rush. Only the twin

.50-calibre machine-guns on the four Polish anti-aircraft tanks remained to drive them back. Exhausted Poles saw Dakota aircraft in the distance, dropping supplies almost certainly destined for them. Then there was a long lull. Near noon, Sévigny's signaller shook him awake; he heard Shermans. An hour later, as the few surviving Polish tanks broke out to meet them, tanks of the Canadian Grenadier Guards broke across the Vimoutiers road. The epic of Maczuga was over.

So was Currie's long battle at St. Lambert. His officers had all been killed or wounded, and the major had to be everywhere and do everything himself. That included knocking out one Tiger tank singlehandedly and directing the fire of his few remaining tanks and anti-tank guns. His handful of men had destroyed 7 tanks, 12 88mm guns, 40 vehicles, killed 300 and wounded 500, and taken an incredible 2,100 Germans prisoner.

On August 21, Simonds finally intervened. Regiments of the 4th Armoured Brigade, now commanded by Brigadier Robert Moncel, were at last sent to rescue the Poles—literally lost on the battlefield. While the Grenadier Guards headed for Maczuga, other tank-infantry teams cleared the road to Currie in St. Lambert and drove south to the other embattled Poles near Chambois. Next morning, men from the British 53rd Division met Canadians near Trun. The Normandy campaign was actually over. It would be fought again many times, but only in the imagination.

THE WAR CONTINUES

On August 20, Crerar's headquarters began planning its share of the advance to the Seine. Behind the weary armoured divisions, the 2nd and 3rd Divisions got ready to pursue the beaten but still dangerous Germans. Though the Normandy campaign was over, the war would continue.

The drive from August 8 to 21 had cost the three Canadian divisions heavily: 1,470 dead, 4,023 wounded or hurt, 177 prisoners, taken almost wholly from 9 armoured and reconnaissance regiments and 22 infantry battalions, perhaps 25,000 fighting men in all. From June 6 to October 1, Montgomery would later report, no divisions in his army group suffered more casualties than the 3rd Canadian. The 2nd Division was next. Those losses, added to a simultaneous toll in Italy where two other Canadian divisions battered their way through the Hitler Line that summer, precipitated the conscription crisis of 1944.

No one will ever know how many men the Germans lost or how many escaped the Canadians through the Falaise Gap. A wounded Kurt Meyer, escorted to safety by a French farmer, found only 300 men and ten tanks left from a division which, on D-Day, had mustered 20,000 soldiers and 150 tanks. The 2nd

Panzer, which had fought its way past Currie's men at St. Lambert, reported on August 22 that it had no guns, no tanks and only a single grenadier battalion. And in the terrible heat that August—temperatures often more than 40°C—the masses of German dead began to decompose quickly and the whole battle area developed a repulsive, fetid stench.

Later, playing the might-have-beens of history, critics would claim that Simonds's divisions had sacrificed a historic opportunity, that the capture or annihilation of two armies in the Falaise pocket would have ended the war. This is absurd. The thin possibility of peace ended on July 20 with the failure to assassinate Hitler. Germany would fight on and no conceivable blockage of the gap could have stopped resourceful, determined soldiers from slipping through to fight and die for their dream of a Thousand Year Reich. As it was, of 100,000 Germans caught in the pocket on August 16, fewer than half escaped; roughly 10,000 were slaughtered by Allied soldiers and airmen and 40,000 more surrendered.

Mistakes were made. Whether Bradley, Eisenhower or even Montgomery should have given the order, American divisions should have pushed north from Argentan on August 13. Depending on two weary, inexperienced armoured divisions to plug German escape routes was unreasonable. Bradley and Patton had left three divisions simply to guard their side of the gap. In the wake of the campaign, colonels, brigadiers and the commander of the 4th Armoured Division lost their jobs as Simonds sought leaders who might not have failed him in Totalize and Tractable. Canadians, as their official historian has claimed, had shown the faults of inadequate and unrealistic training in England. So had British and American divisions.

Yet, like their allies, Canadians had learned the painful lessons of war. They neither were nor believed themselves to be natural soldiers. With time and at fearful cost, they found leaders. At St. Lambert-sur-Dives, Major David Currie earned a Victoria Cross for his inspired and shrewd leadership. Hundreds more, for whom citations were never written, did almost as well in their own battlefield crises. Thousands more conquered agonies of fear to walk forward into the face of death, however reluctantly. They knew that it was a soldier's only way home.

A DAY'S MARCH NEARER HOME

Normandy began the liberation of Europe. It could not end it. The hardbitten German veterans who had escaped through the woods or battered the Poles and Canadians in the valley of the Dives became cadres for fresh SS and Wehrmacht divisions. Canadians and their British and American allies would meet them again in the Scheldt estuary, in the bitter struggles for the Rhine crossings and in the Ardennes offensive in December. Brilliant hindsight told how the war might have ended sooner. Amid the fog of war, Allied soldiers could only struggle forward, meeting hardships and hazards with the soldier's traditional armour of humour, fatalism and profanity.

The Canadians who landed at Juno Beach on June 6, 1944 were almost all green troops, new to war. They paid for their inexperience in blood, but the survivors learned, the generals, majors, lieutenants, sergeants and privates all. They learned how to move silently in the dark, how to dig in to protect themselves, how to co-ordinate armour and infantry and how to make the best use of their artillery. They learned because they had to, and in the process they became a great army. Perhaps General Keller's 3rd Division lacked the ferocity of the 12th SS Panzer Division on June 7; perhaps General Crerar had none of the strategic sense of a Rommel. Those of the Wehrmacht and the SS came from a centuries-old tradition of war and strategy, a tradition that Canadians had fled Europe to escape. The men of the Canadian Army mastered their craft in the crucible of war, and in doing so they destroyed the flower of the German army, arguably the most efficient fighting force in history.

As their columns headed eastward from Normandy, they knew they must be brave for a little longer. Behind them lay the bodies of those who would go no farther. In time, they would be gathered into neat and ordered rows, beneath the ranks of grey Portland headstones that mark their final resting-place. At Beny-sur-Mer near the D-Day landing sites, at Bayeux, where so many wounded died, at Ranville, where the dead of the Canadian Parachute Battalion lie with their British comrades, south to Bretteville-sur-Laize near the Caen-Falaise road, the cemeteries remain, mute and dignified memorials to a struggle that saved freedom in Europe and in Canada, too.

The Canadians who landed in Normandy and the Canadians who fought through Buron and Authie, Verrières Ridge and the Falaise Gap deserve to be remembered by their country. They were not all saints, they were not all heroes. But there were saints and heroes among them, as they fought in the dust and heat of Normandy that summer of 1944. Remember them and remember their achievements.

Brigadier Jock Spragge (right) of the 7th Brigade with a captain from the
Royal Winnipeg Rifles. A tough, able commander, Spragge was typical of the
fine officers Canada's peacetime militia could produce. His black rank badges
were part of the Rifle Regiment tradition the battalions in his brigade shared.
(PA132816/Public Archives Canada)

Montgomery confers with Lieutenant-General G.G. Simonds, II Canadian Corps. Simonds was the one Canadian general in whom Monty had faith. High-strung, aggressive and innovative, Simonds would have his talent tested in the drive to Falaise. (PA129125/Public Archives Canada)

Major L.R. Fulton, a company commander with the Royal Winnipeg Rifles, earned the Distinguished Service Order—a rare award for an officer of his rank. Only time and battle experience could give the Canadians the leaders they needed. (PA131271/Public Archives Canada)

Captain Fred A. Tilston of the Essex Scottish. Despite its ill-starred baptism of fire before Verrières Ridge, the Essex Scottish recovered to become a first-rate battalion. Officers like Tilston—a later winner of the Victoria Cross—helped make the difference. (PA132827/Public Archives Canada)

An aerial view of the crossroads of Lorguichon and the highway from Caen, stretching straight as a die south to Falaise. South of Caen, flat open terrain made observation easy for German gunners posted on the few hills and ridges; any vehicle moving at speed raised a cloud of white dust visible for miles. (PA132914/Public Archives Canada)

A carrier crew from the Toronto Scottish wait for Operation Totalize to begin. The bulges on their helmets are first field dressings, used to patch wounds—the Italian flag fluttering from the water can is harder to explain. As a machine-gun regiment, the Toronto Scottish manned Vickers machine-guns, 3-inch mortars and other heavy infantry weapons designed to back up the coming attack. (PA132831/Public Archives Canada)

Canadian tanks move up for their role in Totalize. The tank on the right, at least, has a veteran crew: tank track has been welded to the bow armour to thicken it and the crew commander is bareheaded, ready to rip off his headset if he has to bale out in a hurry. Survival in battle was a question of trade-offs. (PA132904/Public Archives Canada)

Canadian infantry made history when they began Operation Totalize in armoured personnel carriers, but for most of the battle foot soldiers walked, like these heavily laden Canadians heading past a burning ammunition truck on the way to rejoin their unit somewhere "up front". (PA131375/Public Archives Canada)

A burning truck, victim of American bombers, on August 8 near Cormelles. Victims of the unhappy error lie under a blanket on the right and a grave (or perhaps a convenient slit trench) is open on the left. (PA132657/Public Archives Canada)

Lieutenant-General H.D.G. Crerar (far left), commanding 1st Canadian Army, shows his plans to visiting British commanders, Air Marshal A.M. Coningham, General Sir Bernard Montgomery and Air Chief Marshall Sir Trafford Leigh-Mallory. (PA129122/Public Archives Canada)

Private Leo Benoit of Les Fusiliers Mont-Royal, one of the tough survivors of the Normandy campaign. Many of the French-Canadian soldiers could trace their roots to Normandy, and their accent was easily recognized by the people they had come to liberate. (PA132905/Public Archives Canada)

For his all-armoured advance, General Simonds took the guns out of self-propelled artillery vehicles like this one, roofed them over with armoured plate and created the "Kangaroo". Naturally they were "Top Secret" and photographers had no opportunity to record their appearance. (PA114577/Public Archives Canada)

The standard Sherman tank was no beauty and it was woefully vulnerable to
German tanks and anti-tank guns. It was, however, cheap, mass-produced and
mechanically reliable and it was a vast improvement on the tanks the British
had so far produced. Canadian armoured regiments made the best of them.
(PA132926/Public Archives Canada)

The "Flail" was one of the ingenious adaptations of a basic tank which the British christened "funnies". Its feature was a whirling barrel of flying chains which flailed the ground, exploding mines safely. (PA132875/Public Archives Canada)

Two more "funnies" were mounted on British Churchill tanks. "Fascines" were huge bundles of wood, to be dropped in ditches or narrow streams so that other tanks could cross. The Assault Vehicle, Royal Engineers or AVRE featured a "petard", a stubby-barrelled gun that fired a huge charge designed to

knock out a pillbox. The "funnies" were operated mostly by the British 79th Armoured Division. One of its regiments, a Canadian unit, manned the famous "Kangaroos". (PA116523/Public Archives Canada)

Some impression of the blinding dust cloud is apparent from this photograph of a Canadian Sherman tank advancing. Drivers later admitted that they had merely steered for the dull red orb of the sun. Though they were warned and ready, the Germans unaccountably failed to take advantage of the easy target. (PA132658/Public Archives Canada)

British and Canadian tanks form up for Operation Tractable. In the foreground is a well-camouflaged (but obvious) Sherman. Behind it, towing a trailer full of fuel, is a "Crocodile", a flamethrowing tank designed to burn out enemy pillboxes. In the distance, a cloud of smoke rises from Allied bombing. (PA116525/Public Archives Canada)

OVERLEAF: Vehicles of the 3rd Canadian Division pour forward near Bretteville-le-Rabet as part of the "mad dash" phase of Tractable. The nearby carriers are hauling 6-pounder anti-tank guns of the kind that helped save the Royal Hamilton Light Infantry at Verrières. (PA116536/Public Archives Canada)

By August 17, holding the town of Falaise was vital to the Germans if the remnants of their armies were to escape. Infantry of Les Fusiliers Mont-Royal and
tanks of the Sherbrooke Fusiliers had to fight their way through the old Norman town. It was deadly work. (PA132719/Public Archives Canada)

The massive bulk of a tank gave novice infantry a sense of security—until they realized that the tank itself attracted plenty of fire. In street-fighting, armour and infantry worked as a team, learning to protect each other. Keeping up the pressure demanded discipline, sacrifice and leadership. (PA115568/Public Archives Canada)

OVERLEAF: Devastation in Falaise after the battle. Two women struggle down the main street with their belongings, past the municipal bathhouse. Canadian troops suffered and died, but they did not have to watch their hometowns being demolished. (PA132820/Public Archives Canada)

Lieutenant D.I. Grant took these remarkable photographs—his driver crouches behind a jeep, and a soldier of the Argyll and Sutherland Highlanders of Canada fires at an approaching German convoy at St. Lambert-sur-Dives, August 19. (PA115571/Public Archives Canada)

A few minutes later, as Major D.V. Currie of the South Alberta Regiment, pistol in hand, talks to a French underground member, German prisoners walk forward to give themselves up. Rarely has a photographer been closer to actual fighting. For his role in holding St. Lambert against unbelievable odds, Currie earned the Victoria Cross. (PA111565/Public Archives Canada)

German prisoners of war await interrogation. These include some of the bitter youngsters of Kurt Meyer's *Hitlerjugend* division; very few allowed themselves to be captured. (PA132872/Public Archives Canada)

Canadians from Le Régiment de Maisonneuve pass some of the abandoned
German armour on the road to Vimoutiers. For the first time the Canadians
could sense that the war would end. (PA132813/Public Archives Canada)

OVERLEAF: Major-General Stanislaw Maczek, commanding the 1st Polish
Armoured Division, talks with Canadian war correspondents Lionel Shapiro,
Ralph Allen and J.A.M. Cook. Few episodes in modern war are more dramatic
or heroic than the Poles' stand at "Maczuga", plugging the gap. (PA129140/
Public Archives Canada)

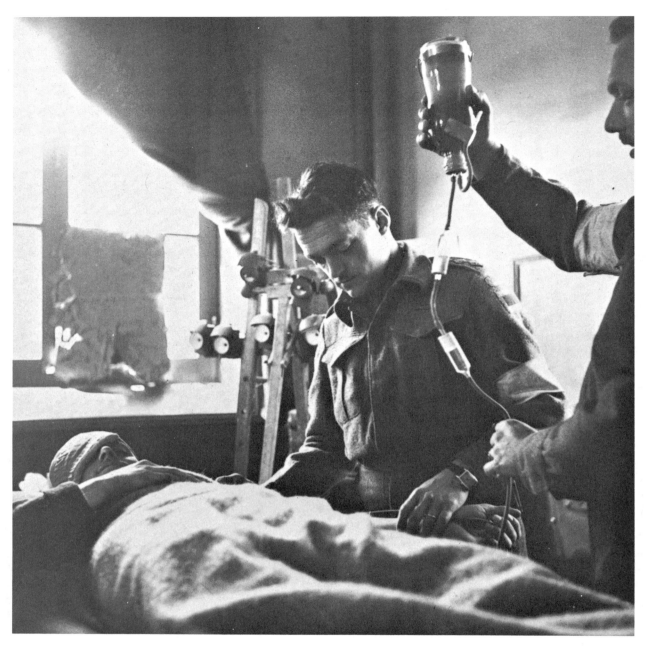

Administering plasma to a wounded Canadian. Medical advances, notably transfusions, sulfa drugs and penicillin, helped save lives that would have been lost in the earlier war. On the other hand, shells, bombs and mines contributed far more to the casualty toll, producing dreadful wounds that defied surgical skill. (PA132723/Public Archives Canada)

Canadian war dead along the road to Bretteville-sur-Laize. It was a bloody victory in Normandy and there was no glamour or glory in a soldier's death, sprawled under an oilskin gas cape or an army greatcoat, rifle and bayonet jabbed into the ground to mark the spot for the burial parties. (PA132907/Public Archives Canada)

German officers, caught in the Falaise pocket, gloomily await orders from their captors. For Wehrmacht career officers, there was an added humiliation in surrendering to the non-professional Canadians. (PA132814/Public Archives Canada)

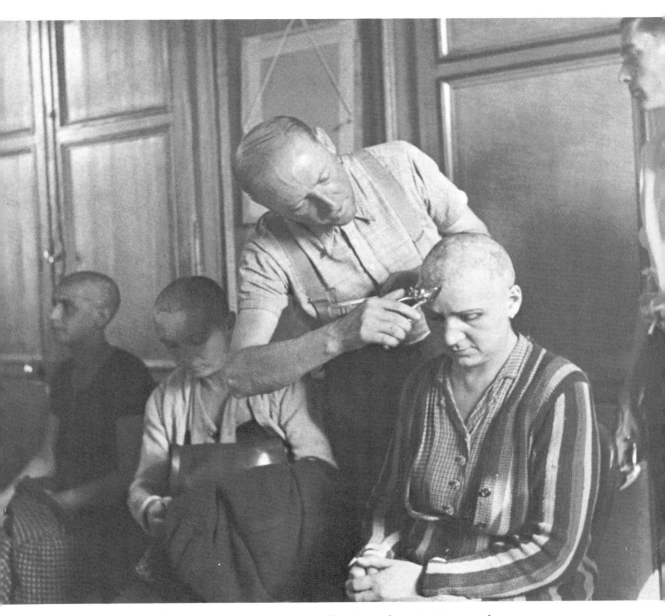

Whatever their feelings about the Germans, few Canadians in Normandy found much to admire in their French hosts. Few acts disgusted them as much as the witch-hunts for presumed collaborators or the shaving of the heads of women who had gone out with German soldiers. It seemed a cowardly vengeance. (PA132815/Public Archives Canada)

A Canadian soldier, dead on the road to Falaise. (PA132906/Public Archives Canada)

OPPOSITE: German soldiers, captured by the Canadians in the drive to Falaise, march down a country road near Ifs. Some had fought to the bitter end; others did no more than their bare duty. Canadians met mostly the former. (PA113654/Public Archives Canada)

OVERLEAF: "When we visited the Canadian cemetery at Bretteville-sur-Orne, where four thousand crosses stand over the graves of those who fell along the road from Caen to Falaise, I asked my daughter Lucinda to notice the ages of the dead soldiers and to remember that they were not the *old* men she had seen at Remembrance Day parades at home. They were kids like her...."—Charles Lynch, *You Can't Print That.* (Veterans' Affairs Canada)

Among
Those Heroes
Present

Out of the hundred thousand Canadians who helped win the bloody victory on the D-Day beaches and in the hedgerows of Normandy, a few hundred won decorations for special acts of leadership and self-sacrifice. None of them would ever claim that only the decorated deserved medals; where so many were brave, decorations went to those whose valour could be identified and recorded for posterity.

Out of the hundreds, we have chosen an arbitrary two dozen, almost wholly at random, to show what Canada's soldiers did in those summer months of 1944. We have chosen colonels and privates, winners of the Distinguished Service Order for officers, and the Military Medal for men in the ranks. We have looked for those whose courage was tested in every kind of role, from medical officer to front-line infantry soldier. Through these brief, understated accounts of their deeds we try to relive the terror and the courage of the battlefield.

We apologize to those we have picked out, for giving them a special and unsought recognition. We apologize to the vast majority whom we have not included—we know that they, more than most, will understand.

MAJOR WILLIAM ROY BRAY commanded the right assault squadron of the Fort Garry Horse on D-Day. Once ashore at St. Aubin-sur-Mer, he found that minefields had stopped the advance and panic was setting in. At once, he pointed his tank at the minefield, ordered the squadron to follow and got through with a loss of only three tanks. Then, he controlled the fire from his remaining tanks so that infantry were helped to their objectives. This kind of determination got the Canadians ashore and won Major Bray an immediate Distinguished Service Order.

As SAPPER WALTER COVEYDUCK, 5 Field Company, Royal Canadian Engineers, sheltered behind the sea-wall on Nan Red beach on D-Day, he saw a landing craft drop its ramps on the beach. Immediately, a huge wave lifted the craft and tangled one of two ramps. As the infantry on board hesitated, Coveyduck ignored the hail of mortar fragments and machine-gun fire, raced across the beach and managed to anchor the ramp with his own body. He remained as the soldiers poured ashore. An hour later, passing a burning Sherman loaded with shells and mines and about to explode, Coveyduck noticed a wounded trooper beside the tank. He and a sergeant grabbed a stretcher, ran over and rescued the man. For two such acts of courage and presence of mind, he won the Distinguished Conduct Medal.

SERGEANT LLOYD WILLIAM CUDDIE, a troop sergeant in the Sherbrooke Fusiliers, was caught by 8 German Panther tanks near St. André-sur-Orne on July 22. Within minutes, 3 Canadian tanks were on fire, 2 were damaged and a sixth could move only in low gear. Only Cuddie's tank was fit for battle. As the Panthers circled to destroy the outnumbered Shermans, Cuddie knocked out the lead German tank. The others turned on him. Cuddie moved his tank to draw fire and to lead the Germans into a position where the damaged Canadian tanks could hit them. With skill, courage and luck, he succeeded and all 7 of the superior German Panthers were destroyed. Sergeant Cuddie received the Distinguished Conduct Medal.

MAJOR CHARLES OSBORNE DALTON was one of two brothers who commanded assault companies of the Queen's Own Rifles on D-Day. Like others, his men soon learned that German beach defences were intact and very dangerous. Though 65 of his men were casualties by the time his company hit the beach, Major Dalton led them to the sea-wall, suffering a severe head wound in the process. He personally laid charges that knocked out a German pillbox, and other men followed his example. Major Dalton earned an immediate Distinguished Service Order.

MAJOR HUME ELLIOT DALTON, like his brother, commanded an assault company of the Queen's Own Rifles on D-Day. He led men of A Company so aggressively that they crushed German resistance on the beaches and drove the survivors into the fields beyond Bernières-sur-Mer. Wounded on D-Day-plus-6 leading his company across open wheat fields at Le Mesnil-Patry, he returned to serve throughout the rest of the war. For his bravery and spirit, he earned the Distinguished Service Order.

On June 11, 1944, CORPORAL PAUL DESBIENS of Le Régiment de la Chaudière found himself and his section cut off and trapped by German fire. Knowing that he had to get back, Desbiens stayed calm and set some of his men to firing and throwing grenades while others slipped back. By coolly managing a tiny but textbook-perfect battle, Corporal Desbiens brought back his 4 men and some vital information about the German defences at Le Hamel and Rots. For this he won the Military Medal.

On August 1, 1944, MAJOR JACQUES DEXTRAZE led his company of Les Fusiliers Mont-Royal to capture the church at St. Martin-de-Fontenay. In the first stage, as German fire swept the open street and his men hesitated, Major Dextraze calmly walked across the street and stood against the churchyard wall, exposed to German machine-gun fire and grenades. With his example, the assault troops braved the fire and crossed the street. Then he led them over the wall and cleared the yard. For winning the church and holding it under savage German fire and assaults, Major Dextraze won the Distinguished Service Order. Later, he served as Chief of the Defence Staff of the Canadian Armed Forces.

ACTING LIEUTENANT-COLONEL CHARLES "BUD" DRURY, of 4th Canadian Field Regiment, directed the artillery fire during the attack on Louvigny on the night of July 18-19. Twice he crawled beyond the advance infantry positions to get a better view of the German defences. During the attack, he ignored snipers and heavy fire to direct his guns. When Brigadier Sherwood Lett was wounded, Colonel Drury took over the brigade and managed the battle with skill and success. For this he earned the Distinguished Service Order. Later Drury became a senior civil servant and Liberal cabinet minister.

At Les Buissons near Buron, Kurt Meyer's SS Panzer Grenadiers began their drive to crush the Canadian beachhead. No. 10 Platoon of the Cameron Highlanders of Ottawa was blasted by mortars, shells and machine-gun fire. CORPORAL GEORGE FRASER manned his Vickers machine-gun and returned the fire. He and his crew were hit. The others were hauled away to safety; he kept firing. Others in the platoon took shelter from the hail of steel; Fraser kept firing even while a second wound bled profusely. Finally the German attack ended, and stretcher-bearers carried Fraser away. For helping save his comrades and the Canadian line, he earned the Military Medal.

On July 20, 1944, D Company of Les Fusiliers Mont-Royal was ordered to capture Beauvoir Farm. LIEUTENANT GILLES GAMACHE commanded a leading platoon. German fire hit many Canadians and the attackers began to hesitate. Badly wounded, Lieutenant Gamache refused to quit. He reorganized both leading platoons, grabbed a Bren gun and took the objective. Then, despite intense German mortar and machine-gun fire, he moved around the position, organizing the defence against the inevitable German counter-attack. Only when the German thrust was repelled was Gamache, now unconscious from loss of blood, evacuated. For his extraordinary heroism, he won the Distinguished Service Order, a rarity for so junior an officer.

When the Highland Light Infantry attacked Buron on July 8, 1944, SERGEANT AUGUST HERCHENRATTER commanded one of the assaulting platoons. He led the way and personally crawled forward to blast a key German machine-gun post with grenades. As his men pushed through to the final objective, heavy mortar fire made them take cover. Each time, Sergeant Herchenratter shouted and waved to his men to keep moving. Finally, with only 6 or 7 men, he wiped out most of a German platoon in a defended orchard. On the objective, he organized the remnant of two platoons—only 19 men—and drove off a strong German counter-attack. His courage and inspiration earned him a Distinguished Conduct Medal.

SERGEANT MOSES HURWITZ was a tank commander with the Canadian Grenadier Guards. During the attack on Cintheaux, during Operation Totalize, he covered his troop commander's advance and then, to occupy the captured position, organized an attack on foot. During the fight, a German self-propelled gun exploded, killing and wounding several Canadians and pinning Hurwitz under a tree. He managed to crawl out. Despite burns and a wound, he grabbed a Bren gun and helped lead the attack, taking 31 German prisoners. His leadership helped take Cintheaux and won him an immediate Military Medal.

On June 9, 1944, CORPORAL EDWARD JONES found himself platoon sergeant of the 1st Canadian Scottish, defending the railway embankment at Putot-en-Bessin as the Germans began a major tank-infantry assault on the Allied beachhead. As his men sheltered from German artillery, machine-guns and the fire of Tiger tanks, Corporal Jones moved from group to group collecting information and keeping his men calm. When the German attack came, preceded by a barrage of fire, most soldiers took cover. Picking up a Bren gun, Corporal Jones jumped to the top of his slit trench and sprayed the advancing Germans. Others followed suit and the attack was beaten back. For his courage, coolness and leadership, he earned the Distinguished Conduct Medal.

When battalion headquarters of the Regina Rifles was overrun by German tanks on the night of June 8-9, 1944, one of the men who saved the situation was RIFLEMAN JOSEPH LAPOINTE. Despite German machine-gun fire, Lapointe ignored his own safety and fired his heavy PIAT at fifteen yards' range, knocking out a Panther tank and a heavy armoured car. He was awarded a Military Medal.

GUARDSMAN JOE LEVITT of the Governor General's Foot Guards was wireless operator in a Sherman tank. On August 9, during Totalize, his crew commander was wounded and temporarily blinded. Levitt applied first aid and took over. When his turret gun hit a tree and broke the traversing shaft, Levitt showed the gunner how to rotate the weapon using body weight. Five days later, on August 14, his was the lead tank of the regiment. When the wireless broke down, Levitt got out of the turret, ignored the hail of shells and bullets and got communications working by holding the aerial together with his hands. By keeping his tank in touch with headquarters, Levitt was "a vital factor in the future success of the Regiment". He won the Military Medal.

LANCE CORPORAL LYLE ALBERT LITTLE of the Royal Canadian Army Service Corps was an ambulance driver. When 11 Field Ambulance came under prolonged German artillery and air attack at Verson on the night of July 16-17, Little ignored the shelling and hauled sick and wounded men from canvas shelters to the relative safety of a nearby house. Then he got to work changing tires and fixing up the jeep ambulances to collect wounded. Next, he set out to find a route for heavy ambulances, located a dangerous shellhole in the dark and guided vehicles past it. His cool efficiency saved lives and earned him the Military Medal.

LIEUTENANT (ACTING CAPTAIN, ACTING MAJOR) IVAN MARTIN commanded B Company of the Argyll and Sutherland Highlanders under overall command of Major D.V. Currie, during the Falaise Gap fighting. With Currie's tanks, Martin's infantry cleared half a town and then dug in to face furious counter-attacks as the Germans tried to break out of the trap. Major Martin twice went forward alone as German self-propelled guns blasted his company's positions, directed Canadian artillery and neutralized the German guns. Returned from the second such mission, he was hit by an enemy shell and mortally wounded. He was awarded a posthumous United States Distinguished Service Cross.

During the attack on the Château d'Aubigny on August 14, 10 Platoon of the Stormont, Dundas and Glengarry Highlanders had bogged down. The platoon commander was mortally wounded; survivors waited for leadership. It came from PRIVATE DONALD NICHOLAS, who grabbed his Bren gun and headed for the Germans, firing from the hip. He disposed of 3 of them; 35 others surrendered and the platoon continued without further losses. For this act of courage, Nicholas earned the Military Medal.

SERGEANT JAMES A. ROMAIN landed west of Courseulles on D-Day. His company of Royal Canadian Engineers was responsible for clearing beach obstacles and Romain got busy without waiting for officers to show up. While he waited for the tide to go out, he organized rescue parties to pull wounded men out of the water and up on the beach. Then he and his men got to work on the obstacles, clearing a 500-yard and a 200-yard gap within an hour. Throughout, Romain was on his feet under heavy German fire and in constant danger of touching off a mine. For his leadership and courage, Romain was awarded the Military Medal.

CORPORAL HAROLD SAWYER was one reason why the Royal Hamilton Light Infantry took their objective on Verrières Ridge on July 25, 1944. As the lead company approached a line of hedges, it was blasted by dug-in tanks and by machine-guns in front. Corporal Sawyer led 3 men out to the right, slipped past the tanks and systematically knocked out 4 successive machine-gun posts. He was wounded but the battalion could push through. He earned a Distinguished Conduct Medal for his skill and courage.

MAJOR EDOUARD WILFRID TREMBLAY, 4 Canadian Medium Regiment, was directing his guns on behalf of the 1st Polish Armoured Division. On August 12, while he sheltered from German shelling and mortars under a Sherman, he heard a Canadian gunner crying for help. Major Tremblay left his place of safety, ran to the wounded man and found the gunner's arm hanging by a shred of skin. Tremblay used his revolver lanyard to make a tourniquet and dragged the man to safety. For this act and his superb professionalism in controlling the guns, he earned the Distinguished Service Order.

On August 20, a German battle group led by Lieutenant-General Erwin Menny, with 750 men, 4 tanks and other armoured vehicles, attacked B Company of the Stormont, Dundas and Glengarry Highlanders, determined to break out. CAPTAIN JOHN WATT, second-in-command of the company, had been sent to look after the anti-tank defences. When he saw that his company was overrun, he organized and led the counter-attack force, a mere 40 men. His courage and leadership inspired his men and led to the capture of Menny and 400 Germans and the destruction of their equipment. Watt earned the Military Cross.

On D-Day, at Bernières-sur-Mer, LIEUTENANT JAMES WHITTAKER, Royal Canadian Engineers, found himself stuck in a landing craft that could make no further progress past the underwater obstacles. Finally, he decided that he must swim to the beach if his technical knowledge was to be available for clearing operations. Unfortunately, he could barely swim, and he had to be brought back in a near-drowned state. Finally the landing craft got to the beach. As men and bulldozers went ashore, Whittaker was hit in the face and neck by mortar shell splinters. Still suffering from shock and bleeding from wounds, he insisted on going ashore and working with his platoon through the rest of the day and night until he collapsed from exhaustion. For his refusal to quit, he earned the Military Cross.

During the 6th Brigade's drive south of Caen on July 20, CAPTAIN GEORGE WODEHOUSE of the Royal Canadian Army Medical Corps commanded a Casualty Collecting Post. Casualties poured in while the post itself was blasted by German artillery and mortar shells. Working in the open without any protection, Wodehouse treated 35 casualties in an hour, administering transfusions and meeting the calls for assistance. For his inspiration to others and for upholding "the high traditions of the Medical Services", he earned a Military Cross.

The Order of Battle
of the First Canadian Army
in Normandy

This is only the skeleton organization of the Canadian formations in Normandy. A host of units, from artillery-locating batteries to ordnance field parks, are not included although they and the thousands of men and women in them were essential to the campaign and their sheer bulk would have told us much about the complexity of a modern army in battle. Included in this list, for reasons that will be obvious to those who read the text, are Canada's closest allies in the final days of the campaign, the 1st Polish Armoured Division.

FIRST CANADIAN ARMY (General H.D.G. Crerar)

Troops Directly Under Command
    25th Canadian Armoured Delivery Regiment (The Elgin Regiment)

1st Army Group, Royal Canadian Artillery
    11th Army Field Regiment
    1st Medium Regiment
    2nd Medium Regiment
    5th Medium Regiment

2nd Army Group, Royal Canadian Artillery
    19th Army Field Regiment
    3rd Medium Regiment
    4th Medium Regiment
    7th Medium Regiment
    2nd Heavy Anti-Aircraft Artillery Regiment (Mobile)

Headquarters Defence Battalion (Royal Montreal Regiment)

II Canadian Corps (Lieutenant-General G.G. Simonds)
Troops Directly Under Command
2nd Canadian Armoured Brigade
> 6th Armoured Regiment (1st Hussars)
> 10th Armoured Regiment (Fort Garry Horse)
> 27th Armoured Regiment (The Sherbrooke Fusiliers)

> 18th Armoured Car Regiment (12th Manitoba Dragoons)
> 6th Anti-Tank Regiment
> 2nd Survey Regiment
> 6th Light Anti-Aircraft Regiment
> Corps Defence Company (Prince Edward Island Light Horse)

2ND CANADIAN INFANTRY DIVISION (Major-General Charles Foulkes)
> 8th Reconnaissance Regiment (14th Canadian Hussars)
> 4th Field Regiment
> 5th Field Regiment
> 6th Field Regiment
> 2nd Anti-Tank Regiment
> 3rd Light Anti-Aircraft Regiment
> The Toronto Scottish Regiment (machine-gun battalion)

4th Infantry Brigade
> The Royal Regiment of Canada
> The Royal Hamilton Light Infantry
> The Essex Scottish Regiment

5th Infantry Brigade
> The Black Watch (Royal Highland Regiment) of Canada
> Le Régiment de Maisonneuve
> The Calgary Highlanders

6th Infantry Brigade
> Les Fusiliers Mont-Royal
> The Queen's Own Cameron Highlanders of Canada
> The South Saskatchewan Regiment

3RD CANADIAN INFANTRY DIVISION (Major-General R.F.L. Keller)
  7th Reconnaissance Regiment (17th Duke of York's Royal Canadian
    Hussars)
  12th Field Regiment
  13th Field Regiment
  14th Field Regiment
  3rd Anti-Tank Regiment
  4th Light Anti-Aircraft Regiment
  The Cameron Highlanders of Ottawa (machine-gun battalion)

7th Infantry Brigade
  The Royal Winnipeg Regiment
  The Regina Rifle Regiment
  1st Battalion, The Canadian Scottish Regiment

8th Infantry Brigade
  The Queen's Own Rifles of Canada
  Le Régiment de la Chaudière
  The North Shore (New Brunswick) Regiment

9th Infantry Brigade
  The Highland Light Infantry of Canada
  The Stormont, Dundas and Glengarry Highlanders
  The North Nova Scotia Highlanders

4TH CANADIAN ARMOURED DIVISION (Major-General George Kitching)
  29th Armoured Reconnaissance Regiment (The South Alberta Regiment)

4th Armoured Brigade
  21st Armoured Regiment (The Governor General's Foot Guards)
  22nd Armoured Regiment (The Canadian Grenadier Guards)
  28th Armoured Regiment (The British Columbia Regiment)
  The Lake Superior Regiment (Motor)
  15th Field Regiment
  23rd Field Regiment (Self-Propelled)
  5th Anti-Tank Regiment
  8th Light Anti-Aircraft Regiment

10th Infantry Brigade
  10th Independent Machine Gun Company (New Brunswick Rangers)
  The Lincoln and Welland Regiment
  The Algonquin Regiment
  The Argyll and Sutherland Highlanders of Canada (Princess Louise's)

Canadian Units serving with British formations:
> 1st Canadian Armoured Personnel Carrier Regiment (with 79th
>   British Armoured Division)
> 1st Canadian Parachute Battalion (with 6th British Airborne Division)

Allied Formations Under Command, First Canadian Army

1ST POLISH ARMOURED DIVISION (Major-General Stanislaw Maczek)
> 10th Mounted Rifle Regiment (Reconnaissance)
> 1st Polish Armoured Regiment
> 2nd Polish Armoured Regiment
> 24th Lancers
> 1st Field Artillery Regiment
> 2nd Field Artillery Regiment
> 1st Anti-Tank Regiment
> 10th Dragoons (Motor)
> Podolian Light Infantry
> 8th Light Infantry
> 9th Light Infantry

Further
Reading

Our most important reason for writing this book is the lack of a fair, accessible history of the Canadian share in the D-Day landing and Normany campaign of 1944. British and American historians, for their own national reasons, have almost ignored Canada's role while the few Canadian books of recent vintage on the war seem to have been preoccupied with the tragedy of Dieppe.

There are two impressive exceptions. Reginald Roy's *1944: The Canadians in Normandy* (Toronto, 1984) is a detailed, thorough, though somewhat uncritical assessment of the Normandy campaign; undoubtedly the fullest recent account. Although designated an "official history", Colonel C.P. Stacey's *The Victory Campaign* (Ottawa, 1960) is lively as well as thorough. While Stacey did not shrink from judgement, even more of his personal reactions can be found in his memoirs, *A Date with History* (Ottawa, 1983).

Thanks to Stacey, the Army was unique among Canadian forces in completing an official history of the war. The Royal Canadian Navy settled for a popular volume, Joseph Schull's *Far Distant Ships* (Ottawa, 1950), on the bizarre assumption of a postwar defence minister that no one would ever be interested in military history. Outside the British official histories of the air war, which seldom pick out the contributions of the tens of thousands of Canadian aircrew, only personal memoirs as yet record the contribution of the Royal Canadian Air Force. An official history is finally making slow progress.

A number of British and American authors have written about the D-Day landings and the subsequent savage battles. One of them, Cornelius Ryan's *The Longest Day* (New York, 1959), became a film in which Canadians were allowed the most minor of cameo roles. The notion that the Canadian landing on Juno beach was a holiday excursion is properly exploded by John Keegan in *Six Armies in Normandy* (London, 1982). This excellent book with a timely message is by one of the most brilliant military historians of our time. Unfortunately, while the book does honour to the Canadians, a number of errors hardly do them justice. Another first-rate British book, the only one to probe the experience of combat, is John Ellis, *The Sharp End of War: The Fighting Man in World War II* (Newton Abbot, 1980).

These to some degree supplant two older but still worthy works. Chester Wilmot's *The Struggle for Europe* (London, 1952) made excellent use of interviews with captured German generals, already presented in more sketchy form by the Canadian journalist Milton Shulman in *Defeat in the West* (London, 1947). Another book which dealt in much greater detail with the Normandy campaign and the crucial role of 21st Army Group was Alexander McKee's *Caen: The Anvil of Victory* (London, 1964). The British soldier Lieutenant-General Sir Brian Horrocks also had much to say about the Canadians in *Corps Commander* (London, 1977), while Nigel Hamilton, in *Monty: Master of the Battle, 1942-4* (London, 1983), reflects Montgomery's harsh view of some Canadian generals.

American books on the D-Day campaign commonly lump the Canadians with the British and offer a few dyspeptic and almost always ill-informed comments on the struggle to close the Falaise Gap. The best and most recent of major works is Russell F. Weigley's massive *Eisenhower's Lieutenants: The Campaign of France and Germany* (Bloomington, Ind., 1981). An American book by Col. Carlo D'Este, *Decision in Normandy* (New York, 1984), insists that Montgomery deceived everyone, from Eisenhower to historians, by concealing the fact that his real campaign plan was a drive through Caen to crack the German front. This book is a reminder of Napoleon's dictum that he would rather fight allies than have them. Most books, British and American, which appeared before F.W. Winterbotham's *The Ultra Secret* (New York, 1974) need to be revised.

Apart from the official histories by Colonel Stacey, a number of recent scholarly studies add greatly to our understanding of the Canadian effort in Normandy. Colonel John English's *The Canadian Army in the Normandy Campaign: A Study of Failure in High Command* (New York, 1991) is a first-class and very critical analysis of the Canadian Army's training and leadership, with its focus on General Guy Simond's inability to use II Canadian Corps to close the Falaise Gap expeditiously. Terry Copp and Bill McAndrew are equally innovative in *Battle Exhaustion: Soldiers and Psychiatrists in the Canadian Army, 1939–1945* (Montreal, 1990), which studies, among other things, the extraordinarily high number of battle exhaustion casualties in Normandy. Copp has also published, with Robert Vogel, *Maple Leaf Route: Caen* (Alma, Ontario, 1983) and *Maple Leaf Route: Falaise* (Alma, 1983), attractive coffee table–size volumes that contain new information on the Normandy campaign. His most recent book is *The Brigade: The Fifth Canadian Infantry Brigade, 1939–1945* (Stoney Creek, Ontario, 1992), a history and analysis of one brigade in the 2nd Canadian Infantry Division that fought its way through Normandy.

Almost all the armoured and infantry regiments, most of the supporting arms and services and some of the smaller units in the Canadian divisions have left histories of their service in Normandy. Some, like the Fort Garry Horse's *Vanguard* or *Le geste du Régiment de la Chaudière*, written by Michel Gauvin and Armand Ross, were published in the Netherlands immediately after the war. Others, like R.H. Roy's history of the Canadian Scottish, *Ready for the Fray* (Vancouver, 1958) or G.F.G. Stanley's *In the Face of Danger* (Fort William, 1960), the story of the Lake Superior Regiment (Motor), were commissioned from professional military historians.

Regimental histories have strengths and limitations as sources. As our book underlines, the regimental system provided much of the strength and cohesion of Canada's soldiers as they fought their way to victory. The regiment was a soldier's family and the histories, though usually based on such vital records as the unit war diary, tend to an uncritical enthusiasm. Rare indeed are the regimental histories which even hint at difficulties and setbacks which are the inevitable accompaniment of war against such formidable enemies as the Germans. An American, C.E. Dornbusch, has compiled a very thorough bibliography of Canadian regimental and unit histories published until 1965: *The Canadian Army, 1855-1965* (New York, 1966).

The saddest gap in the Canadian record of the Normandy campaign is the relative absence of personal memoirs and biographies. The only Canadian general to write his own account was Major-General George Kitching, whose *Mud and Green Fields* (Langley, British Columbia, 1985) is remarkably frank about events, including his relief from command of the 4th Canadian Armoured Division. Less frank, but still immensely valuable, is *The Canadian Summer: The Memoirs of James Alan Roberts* (Toronto, 1981). Roberts commanded an armoured car regiment in Normandy and later rose to brigade command. There are also several recent biographies, most notably Dominick Graham's *The Price of Command: A Biography of General Guy Simonds* (Toronto, 1993), the only detailed examination of Canada's most innovative and impressive commander. Tony Foster wrote about his father, Harry Foster, a brigade commander in Normandy, and SS general Kurt Meyer in *Meeting of Generals*

(Toronto, 1986), while Reginald Roy briefly examined another Normandy brigade commander in *Sherwood Lett: His Life and Times* (Vancouver, 1991). J.L. Granatstein's *The Generals: The Canadian Army's Senior Commanders in the Second World War* (Toronto, 1993) combines a collective biography of all the Army's wartime general officers with chapters on the key figures, including Crerar and Simonds.

Other services have left more memoirs, proportionately. One of the most impressive accounts of service in Bomber Command, Murray Peden's *A Thousand Shall Fall* (Stittsville, 1979), includes his experiences over Normandy. Richard Rohmer, in *Patton's Gap* (Toronto, 1981), leaves an interesting account of his time as a photo-reconnaissance pilot, as well as some strong personal judgements about responsibility for failing to close the Falaise Gap. Hal Lawrence's lively career in the wartime Royal Canadian Navy, told in *A Bloody War* (Toronto, 1979), included time on a destroyer off the Normandy beaches. In *Broadcast from the Front* (Toronto, 1975), A.E. Powley includes verbatim transcripts from the Normandy battlefields by Matthew Halton and other well-known CBC correspondents.

History must be written anew for each generation. As our knowledge grows, our memories are filtered by time and our preoccupations are transformed. Even a decade ago, the secrets of Ultra were still hidden. A generation ago, who would have believed that war crimes could be treated with equanimity? Fifty years ago, who would have imagined that German soldiers would become our allies? History remains the well from which we draw our experience.

Index